ს.

SPACE BETWEEN
THE STARS

ANGELA
MILLER-ROTHBART

texture.
PUBLISHING

Space Between The Stars

First published by Texture Publishing (Pty) Ltd

Copyright © 2025 Angela Miller-Rothbart

ISBN 978-1-0370-3126-7

Editor: Alexia Lawson
Cover design and typesetting: Texture Publishing (Pty) Ltd
Set in Warnock Pro 11.5/17

This is a novel. Only historical events and characters are real. All the other characters are a creation of my imagination.

FOR HENRY
56 YEARS AND COUNTING!

Though my soul may set in darkness, it will rise in perfect light
I have loved the stars too fondly to be fearful of the night.
SARAH WILLIAMS

I knew the power of a single wish, after all.
Invisible and inevitable, like a butterfly that beats its wings in one
corner of the globe and with that single action changes the weather
halfway across the world.
ALICE HOFFMAN

FOREWORD

April 29th 1994

Dear Reader,

It was two days after an election that changed the landscape of South Africa forever.

At the polls, the African National Congress, or the ANC as it is best known, had defeated Frederick Willem de Klerk's National Party to become the government of the day. It was a significant, historic, moment. South Africans of all colours and creeds were able to vote, and long snaking queues at the ballot boxes brought about change.

Nelson Mandela, recently released from prison, addressed a jubilant rainbow nation from the balcony of the City Hall on the Grand Parade in Cape Town. Euphoria engulfed South Africans with the promise of peace.

I was in Stuttafords, a departmental store on Adderley Street in Cape Town, when I stepped onto an ascending escalator as a black woman stepped onto a descending one, running alongside. Her dark complexion – like polished mahogany – and her clear brown eyes were offset by the corn-yellow turban tightly wound around her head. As we moved closer, I smiled at her. She smiled back.

Then we were aligned.

She reached over towards me and stretched out her arms. 'Now we are sisters.'

Tears of gratitude filled my eyes. I was suffused with joy, filled with hope. 'Let the past be past.'

But the past has been stamped onto the soul of the nation and the future is unpredictable.

"The work of memory collapses time" Walter Benjamin

With love

ANGELA MILLER-ROTHBART

PROLOGUE

EMMY

My hand trembles holding the page on which the printed message reads: 'I am coming home.'

Although I have yearned for her to return, I am still reeling from the revelations of my past. My childhood begins to feel like a dream that is crumbling in the light of day. I must be brave. There is no turning back.

Do I want her in my life after my childhood was spent without her? The question torments me. Flame-hot resentment rages through my veins but it is tempered with curiosity.

What drove her to leave me behind? Was her reason for leaving more important than me?

I need to know more about the woman they call Elizabeth.

ELIZABETH 1993

The plane touched down in the cool of the early morning. Table Mountain loomed into an azure sky, dominating the city that lay at its foot.

'Home at last,' Elizabeth sighed. Relief washed over her and she inhaled deeply, filling her lungs with fragrant Cape Town air.

How often she had dreamed of this moment. Just for an instant, she felt like a young girl again.

She drove straight out in the car she had hired. The hum of the motor was the only sound as she drifted in a current of memories.

Faces from the past flashed before her. Years had passed since she had turned her back on the farm and the protective mantel of Ma and Pa, and the Coetzees. Would she still be welcome? Or would she be reviled? She breathed deeply to ease the tension in her chest.

Her thoughts turned to Emmy. How would her daughter react to her once the truth was revealed? Secrets in their revealing, as in their keeping, could tear her family apart.

Her stomach clenched with excitement and fear.

Hours later, Elizabeth drove up the dusty gravel road leading to the farm's gate.

She was struck by how little had changed in the years she'd been away. At the entrance, even the sign – Tweefontein – on the majestic metal gate was the same. The two fountains, which bestowed their name to the farm, stood at the top of the pathway that led to the homestead. They were weathered with age but still stood sentinel over their domain.

Only the mound of freshly turned earth, marked with a simple wooden cross and dwarfed by large headstones on either side, was new, the grave in which her father, Karel, was buried.

She walked along the shady pathway to reach the grave. The cemetery was situated beyond the homestead and was bordered by cypress trees, their sculpted branches reaching up as though in prayer. The names of past Coetzees were engraved on the headstones, many dating far back over the century.

On entering the cemetery, Elizabeth made her way to a rusty iron gate at the far end. Karel's grave was beyond the gate in the burial ground reserved for coloured folk.

The slanting rays of the midday sun filtered through the cypress branches and dappled the plaque placed on top of the grave: KAREL APOLLOS – 1932–1993.

Piet-my-vrous called to each other from the branches of the trees. Their russet feathers flashed between the leaves.

Standing in front of the grave under a sun-bleached sky, she remembered the searing summer heat in the valley and moved her travelling bag into the shade. She slipped off her pale-blue jacket and placed it on top of her bag. Halfmoons were appearing on the armpits of her once-pristine white blouse. It dawned on her that the clothes she had packed in London were unsuitable for the seasons in this valley. The long, fiercely hot summers and short, wet winters contrasted with the London climate that she had become accustomed to.

She returned to the grave and ran her hand across the recently carved plaque. Reminiscences of Pa on the day they parted caused an unbearable ache in her chest; the words that lingered, unspoken, between them, and her shuddering premonition that it was their last goodbye. Memories slowed down her breathing. It felt as though time was suspended and she was a child again. She remembered Pa swinging her up onto his broad shoulders and dancing her around the room. She remembered how he threw back his head and roared with laughter when she strutted about in Ma's high-heeled shoes and Sunday hat. She recalled the feel of his large rough hand when her little one nestled in it, and his penetrating gaze that looked deep into her soul, revealing hidden secrets.

'Would I do it all again?' she mused.

'Elizabeth' a voice called out, shattering the surrounding silence.

She turned to face the woman who was walking towards her with her arms outstretched, and gazed into her face, brown and wrinkled as a walnut.

'Ma,' she gasped. 'Is it you?'

'You're too late Elizabeth. All these years he waited for you, and now you're too late.'

PART ONE

CHAPTER 1

TWEEFONTEIN

1985

The valley lay pale in the early morning light. The dry summer wind carried the promise of yet another brutally hot day on Tweefontein.

Bells tolled across the land.

Sundays always made her melancholy. A veil of quiet seemed to descend on the farm when the pulsating rhythm of life slowed down and the church bells' monotonous chime replaced the chatter and daily activities of the workers. Even the animals slackened their pace, sensing it was a day of rest. After heavy midday meals, the grown-ups scuttled to their beds to nap or to lounge about listlessly, warming themselves in the afternoon sun. Boredom enhanced her melancholy.

A willow tree on the bank of the river that flowed at the bottom of the farm offered up its shade. Emmy turned the bucket she carried over and sat on it. Placing her elbows on her knees, she rested her chin in her cupped palms. The sun dappled intricate patterns on the parched earth and the sun-hardened grass beneath her bare feet. The lure of the cool river water became irresistible. She gathered up her skirt and waded into the shallows, her feet slipping on the smooth pebbles covering the riverbed. The water rippled as she followed it downstream where it cascaded into a deep pool. She peered into the swirling water hoping to catch her reflection, but all she saw was a dark void.

Maybe I don't exist, she mused. The painful certainty in her best friend Marie's voice rang in her ears: 'If you don't have a mom and dad you can't exist.'

She heard the whispers behind her back. They called her Witkind – White Child. The Coetzees, Freda and Dirk, owned the farm and lived in the big house near the entrance. They treated her as if she were their child but even though her skin was the same colour as theirs, they too called her Witkind.

'Emmy, where are you child?' Oumie's voice called out, breaking into her daydream.

She turned around, squinting into the glare. Oumie stood in front of the house, her blue dress shimmering in the sunlight. She had one hand on her hip, the other shaded her eyes.

Emmy waved at her, 'coming Oumie' she called and waded back upstream collecting the bucket from under the tree. She dipped it into the stream until it was full, then heaved it up the embankment towards the house.

Miemie and Karel Apollos – Oumie and Pa – were proud of their concrete house. Unlike the other dwellings on the farm, it consisted of two bedrooms and had an Aga stove. Pa tended the vegetable garden out front and mended the fence with its iron gate. Large, golden pumpkins ripened on the flat corrugated-iron roof, and chickens scattered about, pecking listlessly at the corncobs.

'What took you so long?' Oumie chided. 'Stoke up the fire before you leave for church. Ousis and the family will be here soon. I haven't even begun to cook the lamb curry yet.'

It was time to get ready. Emmy changed into her Sunday dress, the one Oumie bought for her at the farmstall. Oumie was proud that the blue flowers on the fabric matched Emmy's eyes.

Emmy dreaded the times when Ousis and the family visited. The children teased her, calling her Witkind in defiance of grown-ups who forbade it. Today, as on every Sunday, she'd pray in the church that her skin would turn brown like theirs.

A long road wound up to the steepled church behind the town square. Dust and grit crept into her black patent-leather Sunday shoes with their straps across the instep. If Ousis wasn't coming to visit today, Oumie would be walking to church beside her. She always felt safe with Oumie by her side. At the church, fat ladies in their summer dresses and wide-brimmed picture hats clutched their Bibles and stared at her through narrowed eyes in pinched faces. When Oumie accompanied her, she gave them a cold, hard stare back that said, 'Mind your own business,' and they averted their eyes.

Emmy harboured a shadowy memory of when she was little. When day deepened into night and raindrops tapped on the metal roof, Oumie would stitch and darn by candlelight. Then Emmy would lay her head in Oumie's lap, the candlelight shifting the shadows around them. She would see the secrets that Oumie kept in her eyes. Secrets that hid the past, secrets that made Oumie cry and Pa sad.

'Tell me about my Ma and Pappa, Oumie. Why am I different from you and Pa?' she questioned, her voice small in her mouth. Little bits of memories, like fleeting dreams she was unable to hold onto, haunted her. The touch of soft skin and the smell of perfumed hair. The sound of a voice gently humming and the feel of warm breath on her skin. She remembered being gently rocked in strong arms, but she could not remember who held her.

Pa always sat next to Oumie on the couch that he'd ordered for her as a surprise from the Morkels catalogue two Christmases ago. When Emmy asked these questions, he would rub his hand across his face as though he were rubbing away his memories.

Oumie shielded her eyes from the candlelight, 'Don't bother your head with such things Emmy. You belong to Pa and me and that's all that matters.' She smoothed back Emmy's fair hair, her hand lingering on her forehead. 'Maybe when you're older . . .' Her voice faded.

It seemed to Emmy that she'd never be old enough to find answers to her questions.

When her eyelids drooped closed and her head hung heavy in Oumie's lap, Pa carried the sleeping child to her bed, the one he'd painstakingly carved out of pinewood and painted white. As always, he tucked the multicoloured coverlet around her, the one that Oumie had knitted into squares and then stitched together. Pa returned to sit on the couch next to Oumie.

Oumie had been humming quietly to herself to the tune of 'With or Without You' sung by U2 and coming from the small transistor radio positioned behind her on the dresser. She always hummed while she darned.

Pa moved up close to her, his head bowed, his arms hanging between his knees. Sensing his despondency, Oumie abruptly stopped humming and placed the sock she was darning, in her lap.

'Karel,' she said frowning. 'What's bothering you?' She turned down the volume.

'Miemie, we have to tell her,' he replied earnestly. 'She's growing up quickly and she has a right to know.'

'We have been through this so many times before. Why should we destroy her world? She's content living with us. Don't allow her childhood to be shaped by unhappiness.' Miemie's voice cracked with emotion. 'Besides, Elizabeth abandoned her,' she added, defiantly.

'That's not true! Libby asked us to take care of Emmy until she was able to return. It was too dangerous to take the baby with her, nor could she stay here. The laws are evil, and she is known to the authorities as an activist working to bring down the government. If she'd been apprehended, she would have been incarcerated and Emmy torn from her and sent to an institution. She left to protect Emmy, and us too. This country and its laws will soon change. Libby will fulfill her promise to come back for her daughter.'

Miemie placed her hand on Karel's arm, unshed tears glistening in her eyes. In a hushed voice, she pleaded, 'Not yet Karel, not yet. Please just wait a little while longer.'

Miemie and Karel Apollos remained sitting on the couch until the candle burned low. Their closeness was their comfort, each one lost in their memories. Then they quietly made their way to the large brass bed that they had shared for many years.

CHAPTER 2

1953

The first time Miemie saw Karel was at the annual Christmas dance held for the workers of Tweefontein, the largest wine farm in the district. It was the most eagerly anticipated night of the year. Petticoats were washed in sugar water and ironed until they stood out stiffly beneath skirts. Ponytails were carefully cultivated. Stovepipes and white shirts were the dress code for the men, completed by oiled-back hair.

Miemie remembered music was drifting from the gramophone – Frankie Lane singing 'I believe' – when Karel accidentally bumped against her, and the contents of the paper cup she held spilled down her best Sunday dress. It was one Ousis had handed down to her.

She looked up, into the face of Karel Apollos, who stuttered apologies. His large brown eyes were set above sculpted cheekbones, offset by his slick-backed Brylcreemed hair. The white of his starched shirt contrasted with his nut-brown skin.

Miemie felt as though the ground had fallen away, felt her heart springing into her throat.

Embarrassed, Karel dabbed awkwardly at her dress with a pile of paper serviettes. Seeing the funny side of the situation and enjoying Karel's attention, Miemie dissolved into uncontrollable giggles. Her giggles set him off too. Soon they were both laughing so hard they were gasping for air. Then, contritely, as compensation for ruining her dress, he offered to walk her home when the dance ended.

By this time, the older folks had ambled down to the hall, some even indulging in a dance or two. With eyes closed and dreamy expressions on their faces, they swayed to the music recalling their past romances.

When the last notes had faded away and the lights were turned down, Karel took Miemie's hand in his and guided her through the darkened paths to the home she shared with her Ma and Ousis.

The next morning, as she did most days, Miemie set out for the farmstall that was situated beyond the gates of Tweefontein. It was her duty to keep stock of the jars of bottled fruit, homemade pies, and bric-a-brac they sold to visitors to the farm as well as to passers-by.

Her Pa died when Miemie was a teenager. At his funeral in Pastor Apollos's church, she stood between Ousis and Ma in front of the coffin feeling both numb and pain at the same time. Although Ousis was only two years older, Miemie depended on her sister. When tears threatened, Ma said 'be brave' and Ousis squeezed her hand. Ma took in extra washing and Ousis worked longer hours at Dick's Grocery Store to compensate for the loss of Pa's income, but it wasn't sufficient. Miemie left school, hoping to find work that would help provide for the family's needs.

Old Mister Coetzee kindly hired her to run the farmstall. She was proud of the stall. It had a tin roof, a wooden floor, and a shutter in front which she closed and locked at the end of the day. She had a way of charming customers, selling them two boxes of grapes when they had intended to buy one, or a bag of homemade rusks together with bottled peaches. She made sure the fruit and vegetables were displayed to their best advantage, and she hung strings of onions, bunches of carrots, and beetroots from the beams. Boxes of purple and green grapes, picked from Tweefontein's vineyards, were stacked on the farmstall's shelves. The berries glistened with early morning dew. She filled platters with slices of ruby-red watermelon, offering them to customers. They devoured the fruit, the ripe juice trickling down their chins. Miemie beamed with pride when old Mister Coetzee balanced the pounds and pennies at the end of each day and praised her.

It had been a particularly busy day at the farmstall when Miemie finally pulled the wooden shutters down and locked them.

There Karel was, silhouetted against a fiery sunset. Balancing on his stationary bicycle, he waved at her, calling, 'C'mon Miemie, hop on and I'll give you a ride home.'

Miemie pressed her fingertips to her temples to prevent her head from spinning with happiness. She waved back at him.

'Hop on,' he repeated, helping her onto the bike's crossbar.

With her legs straight out in front and her skirt billowing about, she moved into the curve of Karel's arms as he pedalled energetically, pushing against the wind.

The following day the hours stretched endlessly before Miemie. As jittery as a cat on a hot tin roof, she peered into the distance, hoping that Karel would again appear to give her a ride home on his bicycle. She need not have fretted. As she was about to close the shutter, she glimpsed him pedalling furiously along the dusty gravel road towards the farmstall.

He was there the next day and the one after.

It was the season of long evening shadows. The sight of Karel and Miemie cycling back from the farmstall soon became commonplace on Tweefontein.

On the eve of her eighteenth birthday, summoning up his courage, Karel gently drew Miemie into the shadows of the oak tree and brushed his lips against hers.

Lurking in the gloom close by, a figure stood, silently watching.

Pastor Apollos tended to his congregation in the steepled church with enthusiasm and diligence. When a problem arose with a member of his flock, he sought the solution in his well-worn leather-bound Bible, the same one that had been passed down to him by his father and his father's father before him, all being pastors themselves. Pastor Apollos had reluctantly come to terms with the fact that his only son would not follow the career path of his predecessors.

When Karel entered the house behind the steepled church that he shared with his parents and siblings, he sensed instantly that something was amiss. The Bible lay on the table beside a lamp, its light illuminating the open pages. Karel heard the unmistakable little grunting sounds that Pa made when he was troubled. When his eyes grew accustomed to the dark, he saw that Pa was sitting in the corner, partially hidden in the shadows.

'Why are you up so late, Pa?'

'Son, there is something heavy on my heart that I need to discuss with you.'

Pastor Apollos moved out of the shadows and sat at the table in front of his Bible.

Stricken with anxiety, Karel joined him and stared anxiously into his father's eyes. 'What's wrong, Pa?'

'Son, Miemie Baartman is a good child. I know her family as they are members of my congregation. I've noticed your friendship with her develop these past months and tonight I saw you kiss her under the oak tree. Son, I cannot allow you to disgrace either family. If your relationship is to continue, then you must marry her.' The Pastor slapped his hand emphatically on the table, signalling the end of his conversation with Karel.

At his father's words, Karel felt a smile break inside him. With a fittingly serious expression, he replied, 'Ja, Pa. You know I'll always do what you tell me to.'

The following evening, Karel waited for Miemie at the farmstall. He'd polished his bicycle until it shone, and had washed and ironed his best shirt. Miemie, sitting on the crossbar, leaned against him as he strained to pedal up the hill.

'Miemie . . .' he panted, clearing his throat a few times before he continued, hesitantly, 'my Pa says I should marry you.'

Miemie narrowed her eyes. 'Karel does your Pa want you to marry me, or do you want to marry me?'

'Course I want to marry you. I want us to spend our lives together forever and a day. Miemie Baartman, will you marry me?'

Miemie settled into the curve of his body and threw her arms backward, threading them around his neck, Then, stretching her legs straight out in front of her, she turned her beaming face up to a star-soaked sky and shouted aloud, 'Yes, Karel Apollos, I will marry you!'

It rained on the morning of the wedding. Rivulets of raindrops slid down the windowpane. Miemie knelt on her bed, with her forehead pressed against the glass, gazing forlornly at the ominous dark clouds hanging low in the sky.

'Come now, child,' chided Ma. 'Rain is a lucky omen for a wedding day. Besides the sun will come out in time for the ceremony.'

Miemie turned from the window to face Ma. Her wedding gown hung on the door of the old wardrobe that was once Pa's. Although he had died some years ago, the scent of him still lingered on it, triggering memories.

Her wedding gown felt like a dream, one that might fade away if she touched it. Ousis and Ma had pooled their money to purchase the gossamer fabric of lace and satin. Tannie Saartjie had a gift for dressmaking and was a friend of Ma's. She had fashioned the fitted bodice with pearl buttons down the back and had gathered a full skirt that floated around Miemie. It made her feel like a princess.

The marriage of Miemie Baartman to Karel Apollos was a much-anticipated event in Tweefontein, creating a flurry of activity. Women rolled up their sleeves and fired up the stoves. As if by magic, fruit cakes, biscuits, cinnamon buns and vetkoek appeared. Whole chickens were roasted on open flames. Trestle tables set out in the church hall groaned under the weight of platters laden with delicacies. A three-tier pink-and-white frosted cake on a silver platter took centre stage. Children and adults were bedecked in Sunday finery to attend the wedding ceremony in Pastor Apollos's church. Hennie Witbooi, who was employed at Muller's Panel Beaters and a childhood friend of Karel's, was the best man at his wedding. The owner of the panel beaters, Flippie Muller, loaned Hennie a silver Toyota in which to transport the bride to the altar.

Outside the church, the guests waited impatiently for the arrival of the bridal party. Women in wide-brimmed hats and white gloves tried in vain to keep excited children in tow. Men tugged at their collars, uncomfortable in button-up shirts and ties. Fragile rays of the sun were filtering through the clouds when Hennie drove the sedan up to the front of the church.

There were gasps of admiration as the radiant bride emerged. She was accompanied by four little girls attired in pink tulle skirts and flowered Alice bands. Karel stood stiffly at the altar, wearing the charcoal suit he had purchased on lay-by from Burgers Men's Store. He cast sideway glances at the crowd filing into the pews. There was a hushed silence when Miemie entered the church and the organist started up, playing the strains of the melodious 'Wedding March'.

Pastor Apollos intoned the wedding vows, proudly marrying his only son, then invoking lengthy portions of the Bible. Miemie felt herself sway in the warmth of the packed church and her toes begin to pinch in her new shoes., Relieved, the bride and groom knelt to receive the heavenly blessing once a plain gold band was slipped onto Miemie's fourth finger.

The festivities continued until ribbons of moonlight trailed across the night sky and the last guests reluctantly left for home. Hennie drove up to the church in the silver sedan, with a 'Just Married' sign attached to the back. But Karel waved him away, pointing to his polished bicycle leaning against the wall. 'Hop on, Mevrou Apollos,' he said, tilting his head towards Miemie.

She kicked off her wedding pumps, hitched up the skirt of her wedding dress, and clambered onto the crossbar. She leaned into the circle of Karel's arms as he pedalled furiously to their new cottage in which stood the brass bed, a gift from Pa. But, before they cycled away, Hennie had removed the 'Just Married' sign from the Toyota and attached it to the back of Karel's bicycle.

The bride and groom were cocooned in the warmth of their love, but their future was yet unwritten.

CHAPTER 3

On Elizabeth's fifth birthday, Miemie knew that a promise she had made to Karel was fulfilled. It was a promise she made soon after Pastor Apollos had married them in the Steeple Church.

The local bioscope, aptly named Dreamland, gave coloured folk entrance to certain showings only. Many accepted this indignity, although they grumbled among themselves about '*die witmense*' and 'unjust laws. But, like their elders before them, they accepted the humiliation with feelings of helplessness. Although they loathed themselves for tolerating these indignities, they feared the harsh laws inflicted on them by the government. Their lives were a series of opportunities to survive, to feed their young, and to remain on the right side of the law.

But there was a restlessness among the younger generation, the school children who refused to accept the injustices. They shunned Dreamland with its separate entrances for white and non-white patrons. They fervently believed that democracy would be achieved if they fought for it.

The Last Time I Saw Paris featuring Elizabeth Taylor was one of the occasions that coloured people were allowed entry. A few rows were reserved for them at the back of the bioscope, behind those where the white folk sat. Miemie huddled close to Karel in the darkened theatre and felt her heart lurch when Elizabeth Taylor appeared on the screen. She was struck by the star's beauty and gripped Karel's hand tightly. Her eyes widened in admiration as she drank in the vision of the raven-haired, slim-waisted goddess, and she sobbed on Karel's shoulder after the tragic ending.

Dappled moonlight guided Karel and Miemie as they made their way along the pathway under the oak trees that led to their home. In a pool of light, Miemie turned to Karel and tugged at his arm. She declared fervently, 'I promise you that we will have a daughter and we'll call her Elizabeth. She'll be more beautiful than Elizabeth Taylor.'

Karel slipped his arm around her shoulder and smiled indulgently, 'My Miemie, I'm sure you are right.'

When their longed-for daughter was born – the only child they would have – Karel and Miemie named her Elizabeth and doted on her. As the years passed, it became apparent that Miemie's promise to Karel had been realised. By the time she was a toddler, the child's honey-coloured skin, laughing brown eyes and cherubic features made her the acclaimed beauty of Tweefontein. As she grew to adolescence, her beauty was matched only by her feistiness.

As a teenager, Elizabeth started questioning her parents. She was dismayed by their placid acceptance of the humiliating laws inflicted on them by the government.

'Ma,' she confronted Miemie, 'why do I have to sit at the back of the bus when I ride into town with the Coetzee kids? There are many empty seats next to Dirkie and Helene.'

Miemie heaved a sigh of resignation. 'It's because you are coloured and they are white. It's the laws of this country, my child.'

Elizabeth shook her head vehemently. 'I will not accept it. Nor should you and Pa. Helene is in the same standard as me, but the kids at the white school learn much more than we do at our coloured school. I want to go to university and be educated, Ma. I will not wash, iron and clean for the white people like you do. Look how rough your hands are.' She lifted Miemie's hands into her own. 'Unlike you and Pa I will not tolerate this unfairness.'

With these words, the first seeds of dissent were firmly planted in Elizabeth Apollos.

Alarmed by their daughter's revolutionary ideals, Karel pleaded with her. 'Please Libby, do not become involved in politics. The consequences are too dangerous.' The determined set of her jaw caused a spasm of fear to pass down Karel's spine.

That evening, Karel was pensive and quietly watched Miemie knitting on the couch. The lamplight pooled around her. His fingers tapped restlessly on the wooden armrests of the chair he rested in. His thoughts were in turmoil.

Miemie looked up. Frowning, she studied Karel. '*Wat mekeer*? What is bothering you?'

'Miemie, could it be that Elizabeth is right?' His words came out in a rush. 'She wants to fight for change that we failed to fight for. We were too timid, too afraid. We simply accepted the unjust laws. She will not. It makes me feel proud of her.'

Miemie's lips trembled. 'Me too, but I'm afraid, Karel. I am afraid for our child's safety.'

'There's nothing we can do to stop her now, Miemie. She's part of a brave new generation who will fight for what we never fought for,' he repeated. He exhaled, releasing his pain, and turned to face her, 'I feel ashamed that we didn't.'

Karel leaned back in his seat and closed his eyes, relieved to have expressed his torturous thoughts.

But Elizabeth was undeterred by her parent's misgivings. She was aware that there was a restlessness spreading among the workers of Tweefontein. Secret meetings were being held.

Change beckoned.

CHAPTER 4

Robert Booth, tall, slim and fair, had recently arrived from London. He had been brought into the country by anti-government activists to address clandestine meetings being held in the town. These meetings were at the home of David Moses, a lawyer who had obtained his degree at Fort Hare University. On the night of this gathering, the windows were blackened, the room bathed in candlelight and Elizabeth was among the expectant audience.

Robert's speech was fiery, a torrent of words accusing the government of human rights abuses and admonishing his audience for not fighting harder to change the laws and hence their lives. His face was partially illuminated by candlelight, but Elizabeth noted his aquiline features and the severe set of his jaw. She was captivated by the Englishman, swept away by his passion, his implacable conviction. She saw something unexpected in his eyes, a reflection of some part of herself that she could not let go of. When he asked for volunteers to assist with recruits, Elizabeth's hand was the first to shoot up.

David Moses's home became the centre for rallies and meetings attended by the disillusioned Tweefontein workers, and Elizabeth, to Miemie and Karel's alarm, attended each event. Prominent activists addressed these gatherings, conveying to the group the plans that were being prepared to change the laws and spelling out the dangers of implementing these plans.

It was a fiercely hot evening. The warm summer winds blew across the valley and the song of crickets echoed in the still night. Robert Booth had let it be known in the town and among the workers of Tweefontein that he had an important announcement to make and had called an urgent meeting.

In the semi-darkness of David Moses's living room, with the oppressive heat creeping up on her, Elizabeth sat anxiously awaiting Robert's arrival. Sweat was pooling at the base of her spine. There was a stillness among the group, collectively holding their breath as they anticipated his announcement. After a long wait in the hot room, scurrying sounds were heard at the back door and Robert slipped in under cover of darkness. Tremors of excitement rippled through the room when he stood in front of them. His hands were clenched at his side, red-rimmed eyes added to his haggard appearance. Beads of perspiration appeared on his upper lip. When he spoke his voice, was loaded with emotion.

'Our leaders have decided that the time has come for action and have planned a peaceful protest march in the coming week. We will travel by bus to Cape Town where we will be joined by another group of activists. Then we will travel on and go up the mountain pass to the town of Cedarmount. Our protest is against the detention of the principal of the coloured school by the security police and will begin at the top of the hill close to Steeple Church, continuing to the municipal offices. We do, however, anticipate that it will be anything but peaceful. Once the police arrive it could turn violent. We hope there will be no loss of life, but we are aware of the danger. As a result, safe houses have been established along the route. Medics and paramedics will be on hand in some of these houses. I cannot minimise the potential danger, but we do need volunteers to join the march. Are any among you prepared to march along with us?'

His eyes swept across the hushed room. Each person seemed rooted to their seat. In the throbbing silence, it felt as though all the air had been sucked from the room. And then a voice broke into the stillness.

'I will,' said Elizabeth, raising her hand.

'And I will, *ek sal*,' announced Danie Olifant, raising his hand too.

A cacophony of 'I will' resounded in the candlelit room until Robert held up his hand asking for quiet. Overcome with emotion by the group's reaction, he closed his eyes and dropped his head for just a moment. Then he let out a deep, steadying breath and turned to Elizabeth. 'Courage is contagious,' he said, sombrely. 'All volunteers are to congregate here tomorrow night when organisers of the march will give further instruction. Do not speak of this. It could endanger all our lives. This meeting is dismissed.'

Robert stayed behind after the workers had trickled out of the room. The atmosphere was heavy with excitement and trepidation. Voices were kept low as plans for the march were mulled over.

Alone in the empty room, Robert exhaled, blowing out his cheeks with relief. The meeting had gone as planned with no unwelcome visits from the police. But there was a lingering image in his mind of the raven-haired girl with the green eyes who had been the first to raise her hand. It was an image he could not let go of.

Who is she? Biting his bottom lip, he conjured up her face – her chiselled cheekbones and generous lips, the courage that blazed in her green eyes – and he hoped he'd see her again. Then he shook his head in an attempt to dispel all thoughts of her.

But her memory tugged at him, long after he had turned down the lights and left the room.

CHAPTER 5

In the days after the meeting, tension was palpable among the workers as they went about their daily duties. Knowing glances and surreptitious nods passed between them as they counted down the hours to the appointed day of the protest march. They were aware of the brutal retaliation by the security police to protests and marches. They knew that armoured police vehicles, called Casspirs, were driven into protesting crowds, even into school children, and that rubber bullets and tear gas resulted in injuries. But no one could have anticipated the strength and determination that was building among the farmworkers.

The imposing steel-grey mountain ranges were a perfect foil for those who laboured in the vineyards. The women wore brightly coloured skirts protected by white pinafores and matching kerchiefs. On their heads, they balanced woven bamboo baskets filled with the deep-purple or translucent-green grapes picked off the vines. The men, in their loose-fitting white shirts and straw hats, pushed barrows of ripe fruit to the wine presses. The aromatic juice pressed from grapes was sent to cooling rooms to maintain the temperature of the developing wine. Keeping the temperature low allowed the wine to improve with age. The cooling rooms, a welcome relief from the heat, housed the large wooden wine barrels. The heady aroma rising from the barrels permeated the air.

Their duties helped ease the tedious hours until the next meeting, when they expected further instructions to be given.

Finally, it was arranged that in the early hours before sunrise, a bus would drive up to the gates of Tweefontein to collect the workers. It would transport them to the city before anyone on the farm was aware that they'd left. Not all the workers had volunteered, those who had not were sworn to secrecy.

A sense of foreboding was growing in Karel; he sensed the changing mood among the workers and picked up on the tension. As evening closed in, with his unease mounting, his gaze fell on Miemie who was sitting on the couch absorbed in her darning. They'd finished their dinner of tomato bredie at the kitchen table, but Elizabeth had not joined them. Karel always looked forward to the end of the day when he enjoyed the evening meal with his family.

His work was arduous. He steered the heavy tractors through the vineyards all day. His responsibilities as a foreman rested heavily on his shoulders. He was rewarded by the camaraderie among the men. The younger workers admired his competence and followed his instructions, learning about toiling on the land in the relentless summer sun. The evening always brought him a sense of peace. At day's end, he and Miemie would retire for the night in the brass bed, the wedding present from his Pa.

But tonight was different.

After clearing away the dishes, he could no longer contain his anxiety. 'Do you know where Libby is tonight?' he asked Miemie.

She looked up from her needlework, the candlelight flickering shadows across her face. She was surprised by his question.

'She told me she was visiting Sheilah, her school friend. You remember her, don't you? They've been friends since crèche. Why do you ask?'

'There's talk on the farm about secret meetings, and I feel danger brewing,' he said, pacing the room. 'You know how strong-willed Libby is, what she feels about the laws of this country. I'm concerned that she might be involved in something dangerous.'

Miemie put down her darning and looked into Karel's eyes. Fear creased her brow. She placed her hands on her chest, rocking from side to side. 'Today I worked in the kitchen with Katie Plaatjies. She said there were rumours of a white man who's been visiting the farm at night. No one knows the truth of this. I hope Libby's not part of what's happening in secret on the farm.'

Karel sat on the couch beside Miemie and took both her hands in his. 'Don't worry Miems. I'll have a good talk with Elizabeth in the morning. Put down the darning and come to bed, my love.'

That night Miemie slept soundly beside Karel.

But Elizabeth did not appear the following morning, nor the morning after. It would be many weeks before they'd see her again.

The first bite of autumn was evident in the early morning air. All about her, Elizabeth heard the soft sounds of nature, of insects moving, of birds welcoming the dawn. She stood with the other farmworkers huddled around the entrance.

The gates of Tweefontein were shrouded in a grey mist when the bus rolled in. The engine idled until, almost soundlessly, the bus moved off with its cargo and headed towards the city. The journey lasted a few hours. Many of the passengers drifted off to sleep, leaning against each other. They were lulled by the steady rocking motion of the bus as the countryside, dimly lit, slid by.

The mist had dissipated. A pale sun rose in a sapphire sky. The contours of Table Mountain and Lion's Head appeared sculpted against the infinite blue, but the horizon was an ever-changing spectacle of colour.

At a meeting point on the outskirts of the city, a group of activists waited to join them. There was a festive air as they clambered eagerly aboard, greeting each other enthusiastically and clenched fists were held aloft. As they proceeded on their journey, struggle songs were hummed ever louder until their singing reached a crescendo.

The scenery changed when the bus altered course and headed into the countryside. Greenery, lush from the season's first rains, carpeted the landscape The bus snaked up the mountainside, crawling along the narrow pass towards Cedarmount.

The sun had risen to its zenith. The warmth, and the bus's gentle, monotonous rocking had lulled most of the travellers into a drowsy slumber. They were roused when, having reached its destination, the bus came to an abrupt halt. The travellers stretched their limbs, yawned, and rubbed the sleep from their eyes.

Elizabeth had not slept. She remained at the back of the stationary bus while its other occupants were helped down. Last to alight, she took the hand being held out to her and looked up into the face of Robert Booth. Their eyes locked.

The intensity with which he stared at her made her catch her breath.

'Walk with me,' was all he said.

Elizabeth tightened her grip on his hand.

And so began a walk that would lead her into a future that, at that moment, she could not ever have envisioned.

CHAPTER 6

Hot drinks and platters of sandwiches were offered to hungry workers, who warmed their hands on the steaming mugs. The group vibrated with nervous energy as they waited impatiently at the top of the hill in Cedarmount for orders to proceed.

CHANGE IS COMING! was emblazoned on a large placard that Robert held.

He led the way.

Elizabeth walked with Robert.

The marchers, hesitantly at first, congregated behind them, each carrying a placard denouncing the government and President John Vorster.

Emboldened, they strode down the hill jubilantly singing struggle songs. Their courage was bolstered when they approached the municipal office and increased their volume, waving their placards up high. It was just before they reached the police station, close to the municipal office, that the shooting erupted. The police had been alerted and were waiting in ambush for them as they reached the slope of the hill. Loudhailers were held aloft by the men in blue uniforms, who ordered them to disperse.

Then, without further warning, the first shots of rubber bullets were fired at the unarmed, peaceful marchers. Canisters of teargas were shot into the air blanketing them in toxic white smoke.

Mayhem ensued. Screams mingled with live gunshots. The deafening sounds swirled into a cacophony of terror. Some marchers, paralysed with fear, fell onto the ground, and others ran for cover. Those who were able dragged the injured to safety. But the policemen were not yet done. They stormed furiously among the marchers, kicking the fallen and shooting into the air. Their heavy boots trampled the placards, littering the street with them.

Elizabeth had crouched down behind Robert when the shooting began. She did not know how long it lasted. It may have been only a few minutes, but it seemed like an eternity. Bravely, Robert had held up both hands as a sign of peace, pleading 'don't shoot', but his pleas went unheeded.

Then Elizabeth saw him clutch his shoulder, she saw the white cloth of his shirt sleeve turn a deep, dark red. Ashen-faced he swayed, still on his feet. Frantically, Elizabeth grabbed him and propped him up against her slight frame. She tore the kerchief from her head and wrapped it tightly around the wound in an attempt to stop the flow of blood. A mixture of terror and determination engulfed her.

'Robert, lean on me!' she shouted as she half dragged him out of the surrounding chaos. 'There's a safe house close by. We'll get there if you let me help you.'

Stumbling, her eyes smarting from the teargas, Elizabeth guided Robert through the back streets. She'd memorised the route given to them at meetings and was relieved that the map in her head guided them to the safe house on the plan.

The route had taken them to a pharmacy owned by a man called Benny Levy, who had traded in the area for many years and was sympathetic to the cause. When they arrived at his door, he took control. He was tall and heavyset with a florid complexion and a naturally jocular temperament. Horrified by the appearance of the two activists, he drew them inside and guided them to the back of his premises. He pushed a wooden panel aside to reveal a small attic-type room. A naked overhead bulb provided a dim light. In the semi-darkness, Elizabeth made out a narrow cot bed against the back wall. A folding screen provided privacy for a makeshift bathroom. A percolator bubbled softly on a hotplate that stood on a wooden table beneath a window with frosted glass – the only source of natural light and air.

'Let me attend to that wound. It's deep and may become infected,' Benny said, examining it closely. 'It seems that the rubber bullet had a steel core.' Robert sunk gratefully onto the bed. With the deftness of a surgeon – having originally qualified as a doctor – Benny anesthetised Robert's shoulder and removed the rubber bullet. Then he sutured and dressed the wound. Elizabeth stood by, handing swabs of cotton wool saturated with disinfectant to Benny, her squeamishness forgotten.

'Now drink this,' Benny said, handing a glass containing a dark liquid to Robert. It dribbled down his chin and Elizabeth swabbed it away.

Robert was suffused with pain and woozy from the medication Benny had administered. He drifted off into an uneasy sleep.

As night drew in, Benny gave them a meal, then he secured the premises and left for home. Elizabeth sat beside Robert and cooled his clammy forehead with wet cloths. She curved the palm of her hand around the nape of his neck to raise him and held a glass of water to his parched lips. When he'd settled and drifted off again, she too fell asleep on a mat on the wooden floor beside him. Throughout that night and the following day and night, Robert drifted in and out of consciousness. Elizabeth remained at his side, tempting him to eat and drink while Benny attended to his wound.

The news of the march in Cedarmount and the police onslaught had spread like wildfire. The media's screaming headlines informed the country of the injured and arrested. Demonstrators were denounced as communists; their leaders were sought mercilessly by the government and police from the special branch. Robert Booth, a well-known activist and organiser of countless uprisings, was being pursued aggressively. Chilling tales circulated of cruelty meted out to leaders in captivity.

Back on Tweefontein the news was electrifying. A veil of fear descended on the small community. Many of the workers had not returned.

Karel and Miemie remained indoors.

'I know that Elizabeth will contact us,' Karel said reassuringly, attempting to pacify Miemie. 'She's waiting for the dust to settle. Our Libby is a smart girl. No news is good news.' His words did not appease Miemie who huddled into the couch, her eyes half closed. She willed herself to prepare coffee and sandwiches at mealtimes. She felt turned to stone.

Karel paced agitatedly, continually peering through the window with the hope of a messenger arriving at his door bringing news of Elizabeth. He didn't have long to wait.

A messenger winged his way towards the house.

Along the untarred back streets leading out of the city, a light-grey Vauxhall raced towards Tweefontein. Dusk had faded into night. David Moses sat hunched behind the wheel. Fearing roadblocks, he'd taken a seldom-used detour. The hum of the motor was the only sound that intruded into the stillness of the world around him. He had dimmed the headlights; their light cast eerie shadows.

His heart hammered in his chest. He knew there was a heavy price on his head and the police were on high alert to arrest him. He gave a deep sigh of relief when the lights of Tweefontein twinkled in the distance, beckoning him. 'Almost there,' he murmured to himself.

When he reached the farm, he switched off both the engine and the headlights and climbed out of the car. He opened the heavy gates, pushing against them with his shoulder. A waxing moon offered a little illumination to guide him across the farm fields to the Apollos's house. David crept around to the back and gently tapped on the kitchen window.

Karel and Miemie had fallen into an exhausted sleep, leaning against each other on the couch. The tapping grew louder and startled Karel out of sleep. He prodded Miemie. 'There's someone at the kitchen window. Be very quiet,' he instructed her.

Stealthily, he crept towards the sound of the tapping. Flattening himself against the wall, he peered sideways through the window and gasped with relief. His face was wreathed in smiles when he recognised the figure of David Moses silhouetted in the milky moonlight. David was a well-known lawyer in Malansdorp and had assisted Karel with Pastor Apollos's will when Pa died suddenly of a heart attack.

Karel unlocked the back door and pulled David inside, embracing him before leading him towards Miemie, who was still drowsy. She sat stiffly on the couch, trying to make sense of the progression of the events. David was fatigued with anxiety from the daunting trip. He sank gratefully onto the couch. Miemie, now fully alert, flamed the gas hob to boil the kettle while she prepared sandwiches. They plied David with questions. Sitting on either side of him on the couch, their words tumbled together in their eagerness to know about Elizabeth.

'Where is she?' and 'how is she?' were the most repeated questions they asked while they waited for the kettle to sing.

David spoke urgently and answered the anticipated questions. 'Elizabeth is unharmed and is in a safe house. I cannot divulge more details but you should be proud of your daughter. She's brave. I have a note from her, it has been passed to me through our network of undercover agents.' He handed Karel an envelope.

'What are your intentions?' Karel frowned.

'I'm going to sleep here on your couch for an hour or two, and then head out before sunrise. I'll be met along the way by numerous pickups and will, hopefully, be escorted safely to the border and out of South Africa. I'll be in exile until there's a change of government. It will come about sooner than you expect.' He yawned deeply, settling against the soft pillows Miemie had put behind him.

David ate the sandwiches and drained his cup. He lay down on the couch and almost immediately fell into a deep sleep. Miemie covered him with a light blanket and blew out the candle.

In their bedroom, Karel and Miemie slit open the envelope and scanned the note impatiently. It read: *I'm sorry to have missed your birthday, Pa, but I'm certain to be there to celebrate Ma's. I hope you are well. I am too.*

It was unsigned.

A stab of pain pierced their hearts when Elizabeth's parents realised that it would be some time before they would see her again.

CHAPTER 7

In the room at the back of Benny Levy's pharmacy, Robert was beginning to recover. The morphine fog that had kept him barely conscious was clearing. While drifting back into awareness, he held onto the image of Elizabeth. His memory was like bits of old photographs that fluttered around, reminding him that it was she who cared for him and was constantly at his side. Slowly he lifted heavy lids and whispered, 'Elizabeth?'

'Hello Robert,' she said. 'It seems you are awake at last.'

'How long have I been here?'

'Five days.'

She moistened his parched lips and stroked his forehead. He turned to face away from her, but not before she saw a tear squeeze out the corner of his eye and slide down his cheek.

'You've been on the edge of my dreams,' he murmured drowsily, before slipping back to sleep.

As the hours passed and Robert became more alert, Elizabeth was able to fill him in with the events of the past days. Apart from the shooting and the ensuing pandemonium, Robert had only a splintered memory. Horrified, he listened to her recount what had happened.

A familiar rap on the wooden partition announced the arrival of Benny, who pushed it aside and entered, chortling gleefully when he saw Robert propped up against the pillows with colour returning to his cheeks.

'So, you are back with us, Robert.' He examined the wound and announced jocularly, 'You'll live.'

Then Benny pulled up a seat and studied the pair. He spoke solemnly. 'There have been too many unwelcome visitors at the pharmacy lately and too many questions being asked. We have to get you out of here and to another safe house. Robert, now that you are recovering we need to act quickly.'

Before they could question him, bells attached to the pharmacy entrance tinkled loudly. 'Let me investigate,' he said. 'Turn out the light and be very quiet,' he added softly over his shoulder as he stepped out, replacing the wooden panel firmly.

Commissioner Piet Brand stood menacingly in the doorway, arms akimbo. He demanded to speak to Benny.

'Hello Commissioner,' Benny greeted him affably. 'Is there a problem? Is your baby daughter's ear still causing her pain?'

'Levy, I have reason to believe that you're harbouring communists,' he said, breathing heavily.

Horrified customers backed away as the commissioner strode up, his face only a few inches away from Benny's.

'What?' Benny answered, in mock surprise. 'I would never get involved with that bunch of thugs. You're welcome to look around,' he added, with more conviction than he felt.

Brand's narrowed eyes swept the room, then he glared at Benny and stabbed a finger at him. 'I'll be back soon. You're being watched, take this as a warning.'

The bells tinkled loudly again as Commissioner Brand slammed the security gate shut behind him.

CHAPTER 8

That night, the space behind the wood panel was crowded. Five figures sat crouched on the bed or sprawled on the floor. A dim light cast dancing shadows onto the walls. The tension was palpable.

Sipho Bantu and Barney Stern had slipped undetected into the pharmacy and then into the room sheltering Robert and Elizabeth. The men had come in the busy evening hours, mingling easily with the crowded shoppers, and had evaded the ever-watchful eyes of undercover policemen hovering around the premises.

Benny was the fifth member of the group and had provided coffee and samosas for what was going to be a long night. A plan was being devised to move Robert and Elizabeth from the pharmacy to another place of safety, far from the prying eyes of Commissioner Piet Brand. During the night, the plan was revised many times until all five were satisfied that it was safe to implement.

The birds had begun their dawn chorus by the time Sipho and Barney slipped out into the fading night's shadows.

Benny turned to leave, yawning deeply. 'I'll miss you both,' he said 'but I'll be on hand to help you until you leave. Now try and get some sleep.'

The panel slid into place behind Benny. Alone at last, Robert and Elizabeth fell into a troubled sleep. She lay curled against the warmth of Robert's body in the cavity of the narrow bed.

When the light of a new dawn brushed the mountain tops with gold, the air trembled with nervous anticipation in the room behind the pharmacy.

Elizabeth was carrying out the first stage of the plan hatched the evening before. She tinted Robert's blond hair a darker shade. A navy suit, striped shirt and shiny black shoes replaced the clothes he'd worn before. Eyeglasses and a dark false beard completed his disguise. A wallet, placed in the jacket pocket, contained a passport, business cards and hotel reservations for Bruce Sheldon, a businessman from the United Kingdom. A set of car keys was also placed in the pocket. Elizabeth was amazed by the transformation.

A chaotic rush hour would provide the perfect foil for Robert to slip away undetected from the pharmacy.

He held Elizabeth in his arms for a fragment of a moment before he stepped away from their sanctum. Both had acknowledged the powerful bond that had grown between them, but neither could tell whose tears wet Elizabeth's cheeks. Then the panel slipped back into place and Elizabeth was left alone with only her disturbing thoughts to accompany her throughout the long night.

Benny had placed signs in the pharmacy window offering free toiletries to all customers who purchased any item in the last hour of that day. In the resulting pandemonium, Robert walked calmly away from the premises and climbed into a light-blue Toyota parked under a large shady tree.

The ignition key turned effortlessly. The engine shuddered, then sprang to life and Robert sped off into the night. After navigating the precarious mountain pass, he reached the highway and the thumping beat of his heart slowed down. He was exhilarated by the success of his escape as he headed on to begin the next stage of the plan.

Extra precautions had been taken.

The parking attendant expected Robert and stood to attention when the Toyota arrived at the entrance to the Cliffside Hotel. Robert rolled down the passenger window and leaned across. 'Hello George,' he said, as instructed. 'How's your mother doing?'

'She is well, sir. Thank you for asking,' George said. 'Your underground parking bay is number 23.'

A battered grey Mini was parked in Bay 23. Bruce Sheldon, a businessman from the United Kingdom, sat behind the wheel. When Robert arrived, Bruce slipped out of the Mini and a swift exchange was made. Other than a surreptitious nod, nothing passed between them.

A driver's license, with its photograph of Robert, was placed on the Mini's front seat. Robert had left the passport and the documents he had been carrying on the seat of the Toyota. He adjusted the seat of the Mini, switched on the ignition and flipped the gears, then sped out into a starlit night. His destination was a deserted cottage in a sparsely occupied fishing village, far away from the nearest town.

CHAPTER 9

The following morning Elizabeth woke at dawn from a dreamless sleep. Somewhere in the distance a rooster crowed. All night she'd lain curled up on the narrow bed.

She rose, straightened her cramped limbs, and splashed cold water on her face. The hours stretched endlessly before her. She was tormented by the waiting, not knowing if Robert was safe. Her longing for him made her chest ache. She paced the small room or lay curled up on the bed staring at the ceiling. She felt lonely and abandoned.

Sunlight was streaming through the small attic window when a rapid knocking on the outside of the wood panel startled her. Benny's beaming face appeared in the partial opening; it was accompanied by his thumb held high above his curled fingers. When he entered, she saw that he carried a tray of freshly scrambled eggs and a mug of coffee. Relief surged through Elizabeth and she felt her knees buckle. She fell heavily onto the bed and covered her face with her hands.

'Robert's safe, Elizabeth,' Benny said, sitting beside her and stroking her arm to soothe her. 'All has gone according to plan. Now it's your turn. Everything you'll need is in this parcel.' He handed her a brown-paper carrier. 'Wait until this evening because I'm having another sale to fill the store. We've been through your instructions so many times – are you confident you can carry them out?'

A quick smile and nod from Elizabeth assured him.

Benny disappeared behind the wooden panel and left Elizabeth alone, once again.

The hours dragged by. She fell asleep but woke with a start when the lengthening shadows indicated the approach of evening.

Elizabeth opened the parcel Benny had left with her and spread the contents onto the bed. She slipped a worn brown worker's overall over her clothing, and wound the matching doek tightly around her head, pulling it low over her brow to conceal her long hair. Lastly, she tied an apron around her waist and slid her feet into a pair of shabby slippers.

Slipping a shopping bag over her shoulder she gazed into the hand mirror, satisfied with the change in her appearance. More confident now, she emerged from behind the wood panel and stepped into the pharmacy, blending in with the shoppers. She rummaged through the shopping bag and found silver coins and some notes left for her in a wallet. After she'd bought a few items, she nonchalantly and unobserved strolled out of the pharmacy towards a bus stop, as instructed.

The wait for the bus was agonizing. When it finally arrived, she clambered on board and joined the jostling passengers. Only when she had squeezed onto a corner seat at the window did she feel her shoulders slump and her roaring heart slow down. She watched the streetlights flash by as the bus picked up speed, leading her away from Benny Levy's pharmacy and away from Cedarmount.

Back in Cape Town, the bus rounded a corner in Strand Street, and Bus Stop 64 came into sight. The bus drew to a halt.

Climbing down, she acknowledged with a sigh of relief that the first stage of her escape had been successful. A white minibus with blackened windows was parked on the opposite side of the road. Gingerly, she crossed the road and approached the driver's window. She tapped against it. It rolled down.

'How is your mother?' she asked, according to her instructions, swallowing nervously.

A broad smile displaying perfect white teeth lit up an ebony face. 'My name is Thabu, I am a friend.' He leaned over and slid open the side door of the minibus. She climbed inside hesitantly and the doors whooshed shut. Her mouth felt dry from uncertainty and fear. Only when she was seated inside did he start the motor. The headlights carved circles of light into the surrounding darkness.

He glanced at her in the rear-view mirror. 'You can relax now. You've done well and carried out your instructions to the letter. We were worried about you, being so young and inexperienced 'n all. You must be hungry,' he added as an afterthought and handed her an egg sandwich wrapped in greaseproof paper. She tore off the wrapper, savouring the taste of the nutty brown bread, and licked the last crumbs from her fingers.

'Where are we heading and where's Robert? I was not given any information although I did ask Benny.'

'We withheld the information for security. Now that we're safely out of the city, I can divulge that Robert is in a cottage close to Simonstown. We should be there within an hour, but will likely stop to pick up passengers along the way. Keep the documents in the shopping bag at hand in case of a roadblock, although I hope this won't happen.'

The approach of night and the gentle swaying of the bus made Elizabeth drowsy. Although Thabu kept up a continuous patter, she felt her eyelids droop. The minibus stopped occasionally for passengers to embark or climb down, but there were no roadblocks.

'Seems I have evaded the roadblocks tonight,' Thabu muttered through clenched teeth as they hurtled on towards their destination.

The moon hung low in an inky-black sky. It cast trails of shimmering light across the ocean.

The minibus slowed down and then ground to a halt. Thabu turned off the headlights but left the engine idling. He turned and gently prodded Elizabeth, rousing her out of sleep. 'We've arrived. You're safe now.'

She rubbed her eyes and tried to make sense of where she was. Events of the past few hours seemed like a part of a dream.

'I need to leave now.' Thabu climbed down and opened the side door. 'Robert's expecting you.'

Elizabeth stepped out into the night. With a quick wave, Thabu sped off in a cloud of dust, leaving Elizabeth alone on the beach.

She heard her name being called.

Robert stepped out of the night's shadows. Elizabeth walked into his outstretched arms. He held her so close she could feel his heartbeat. 'You're here at last.' He heaved a deep sigh of relief. 'I have missed you.'

She saw the longing in his eyes and, reaching up, touched his face, her fingers lingering on his skin.

They were alone on the deserted beach, the only sound the gentle lapping of the waves on the ocean edge. Elizabeth felt as though they were the only two people in the world. Robert held her hand and steered her towards a cottage with a thatched roof squatting on top of whitewashed walls. Inside, roughly hewn wooden furniture stood on a bare floor. The table in the middle of the room held large bags filled with provisions, indicating a long stay. Garments intended for Elizabeth hung on a rope rail slung across the wall. It was a simple dwelling, used only by fishermen.

Elizabeth turned to Robert, and her forehead wrinkled. 'How long will be staying here?' she asked anxiously. Her concern for Karel and Miemie was mounting. She needed to contact them.

'Many marches are being planned,' he shrugged. 'We're expecting the government authorities to focus on these marches, among other planned events. It should be safe to leave here within a few weeks. Headquarters will contact me to confirm this.'

CHAPTER 10

The days slipped by.

They waited for a message that would recall Robert to London, a message that would end their idyllic days spent in the warmth of early autumn sun. They strolled along the soft sandy shore and splashed in the ocean, the sea salt drying to a crust on their sun-kissed bodies.

Fishermen had been posted along the coast for their protection and to warn them of any unwelcome visitors. The boats pulled onto the shore daily; the nets filled with their haul of fish.

In the tranquillity of dusk, Elizabeth and Robert joined the fishermen. They roasted fish over coals that glowed on the darkening beach. They ate the succulent, crispy fish in sticky fingers until only the bones remained. When the first stars appeared, Solly, the head fisherman, would start up his accordion and the little group swayed to the rhythm of the soulful music until night closed in.

It had been a balmy day. The setting rays of the late afternoon sun gilded the sky. Robert and Elizabeth ambled hand in hand along the water's edge.

Robert stopped abruptly and turned to her, cupping her face in his palms. 'Elizabeth,' he said, gently. 'I received a message from headquarters. It arrived this morning wrapped in the newspaper together with the fish that Solly delivered. I'll be going back to London and you'll return to the farm.'

Alarmed, Elizabeth gazed at him, her eyebrows raised, questions forming rapidly. 'When?' she whispered, looking stricken.

'Day after tomorrow. Thabu will collect you from the cottage and drive you to the bus that will take you back to Tweefontein. He'll also deliver an airplane ticket for my flight, which leaves for London the following evening.'

Elizabeth knuckled away the tears in her eyes.

Robert fell to his knees in the sand pulling her down with him. He spoke earnestly. 'It seems we've lived our lives searching for each other. Your bravery and your rebelliousness have left an imprint on my heart. Because of this country's laws, we cannot live together or be married here, but we can in London. I promise you that I will come back for you.'

His words gave Elizabeth a throb of hope, even as her heart whispered 'beware'. She sat on the cool sand with her arms looped around her bent knees. A sea breeze whipped her hair. She stared out at the dark sea with a whimsical look in her eyes. *But will I always inhabit the space between the stars?*

The rising moon dappled their entwined limbs, cinnamon and cream, under a silvery light. The night breathed its magic.

By morning, the shifting sands had covered all traces of the lovers, as though they had never made love under a star-studded sky on a deserted beach.

It was a sullen morning. The sky hung low and grey when Robert and Elizabeth stepped out of the cottage. They both wanted to delay as long as possible the moment that she would leave and they would go their separate ways.

Thabu was waiting behind the wheel of his minibus, the engine idling.

'I'll be back Elizabeth,' murmured Robert, as he tilted her face towards his.

Elizabeth heaved a sigh of resignation, 'And I shall be waiting for you, however long it takes.' She turned and walked towards the waiting bus. The force of Robert's gaze when she turned back would be a haunting memory in the long, waiting days that were yet to be.

They travelled in silence most of the way to Cape Town. Elizabeth, lost in her troubled thoughts, was huddled down in her seat, her arms folded tightly across her chest.

The early morning traffic was heavy and Thabu concentrated on navigating his vehicle across the traffic lanes.

In Strand Street, at Bus Stop 64 a bus waited for passengers to board. It would transport Elizabeth back to Tweefontein. Hurriedly, Thabu assisted her, settling her into the back section that was reserved for coloured and black folk. Then he climbed into the minivan and steered it back into the thick of the traffic.

Again, Elizabeth was alone.

Arriving at the farm, she climbed off the bus and was surprised to see how the landscape had changed since she'd left on that foggy morning so many weeks ago. The leaves on trees and vineyards had magically turned to vibrant hues of orange, gold and crimson.

She walked through the gates of Tweefontein along the familiar path leading to her home. Pietman Latief, sitting high up in the branches of an oak tree collecting acorns for pig fodder, first spotted her. '*Sy's terug,*' he called out excitedly.

Pietman's cries alerted the workers in the fields and the news of her arrival spread quickly. They downed tools and joined her along the path, the littlest children running ahead. Karel stood waiting at the cottage door, beaming, his arms outstretched.

'Miemie,' he called and turned back to where she stood, 'Set another place at the lunch table. Our girl is home.'

Elizabeth's arrival back at Tweefontein caused ripples of excitement among the workers. Rumours abounded. Mostly they were centred on a foreign white man. Whispering groups parted as she passed them by, but Elizabeth walked on, head held high, refusing to divulge anything. The more she clammed up, the more creative the rumours became. But those who knew the truth smiled encouragingly, often squeezing her hand.

Miemie and Karel were overjoyed to have their daughter back home. They respected her reluctance to provide any information and resisted the temptation to prod her for details.

The rains had come to Tweefontein. Heavy black-bottomed clouds rolled in from the north bringing torrential rain that soaked the earth. The wind howled through bare branches and the livestock cowered in their pens. Sheets of lightning tore across the sky.

In the gloom of one wintery evening, Karel and Elizabeth were seated at the kitchen table. Miemie stood with her back to them. She was at the kitchen stove, vigorously stirring a pot of bean soup that would accompany a bobotie for their evening meal.

Karel cleared his throat a few times before addressing Elizabeth.

He spoke falteringly. 'Ma and me, we both . . . we respect your privacy and we trust you to make the right decisions.'

Miemie placed bowls of soup on the table and sat down to join them. She nervously twisted the spoon she held. 'My madam, Misses Coetzee, mentioned this morning that the crèche at the church needs a carer because Misses Tobias is in hospital. It's the same crèche that you once attended.' Taking a deep breath, she added, earnestly, 'Would you help, Libby?'

Elizabeth kept her hands folded in her lap. She had a faraway look on her face. Listlessly, she pushed the spoon around the bowl of soup pretending to eat

Karel and Miemie watched her anxiously, alarmed by her diminished appetite.

Elizabeth sighed. She shrugged her shoulders. 'Ma, tell Tannie Freda that I'll be at the crèche tomorrow morning and will help until Misses Tobias recovers.'

For Elizabeth, it felt like darkness had closed in on her as she watched the clock, like treading water, waiting for a message from Robert. Concern for him intensified her loneliness. He occupied all her thoughts. The weeks since their parting at the fisherman's cottage seemed so long ago.

She embraced the opportunity of filling the long, monotonous wintery days and ending her malaise. The following morning Elizabeth trudged to the church's creche. Soaking rains had turned the gravel to mud. Tending to the children brought a welcome release from the despairing thoughts that overwhelmed her. The little ones' laughter and songs brought energy and light to her when she sang and danced with them.

But the weeks passed by with no word from Robert.

Frosty air condensed her breath to fog when Elizabeth set off at dusk for home. She wound her scarf tightly around her shoulders and dug her hands deep into the pockets of her coat.

At the cottage, the sight of an unfamiliar white station wagon at the front gate stopped her in her tracks. She shivered with apprehension, and hesitantly opened the front door, peering guardedly into the room.

Elizabeth was unprepared for the scene that greeted her. Barney Stern was seated at the table between Miemie and Karel. She recognized him by his auburn hair. All three heads were thrown back in gales of laughter, Karel slapping his thighs. Barney's rounded belly shook with merriment., Hearing the door open, their eyes turned to Elizabeth who stood framed in the doorway.

Barney jumped up to greet her. 'I met your parents while waiting for you,' he said and wiped tears of laughter from his eyes. 'I introduced myself as a friend of yours.'

Karel nudged Barney's shoulder playfully. 'He's been telling us stories of his escapades while growing up in Doornfontein,' he spluttered, dissolving into laughter again.

Relieved, Elizabeth smiled happily at the trio. She noted the plate of fresh buttermilk rusks and that the porcelain cups and saucers – the ones Ma kept in the box on the top shelf of the kitchen cupboard – were displayed on the table. The tea set had been a present from her Ma when she married Pa and was used only for special occasions. It seemed that Barney's visit was such an occasion.

Barney's arrival caused her heart to leap with hope that he'd brought a message from Robert.

She leaned in to kiss Ma and Pa and gave Barney a quick hug while gauging his features for a sign, but his face remained inscrutable.

'*Is jy koud, my kind?*' asked Miemie. 'You look cold. A cup of tea will warm you up.' She stood to put the kettle on the stove and fussed about the table, pouring tea and replenishing rusks. Then, smoothing down her apron, she settled back onto her seat.

Elizabeth noted that the fine lines of worry that had recently etched her parents' brows appeared softer now, as they enjoyed Barney's visit.

When the teacups were drained and only crumbs remained on the plates, Barney prepared to leave.

'Stay for dinner,' coaxed Karel.

Barney lifted his palms, refusing. 'It's late and I need to be on my way.' He thanked Miemie and Karel and, tilting his head, beckoned Elizabeth to follow him.

On the doorstep, he put his hands on her shoulders and turned her squarely to face him. 'I've received a message from headquarters in London. Robert arrived as planned and is back at his legal firm. David Moses has also reached London. He asked me to bring this message to you. Under no circumstances are you to contact Robert or him, not until the dust settles. We need to protect you. Only contact them if it's necessary.' He handed her a sealed envelope. 'An emergency number is inside. Robert intends to be back in Cape Town as soon as it is safe. Right now, the situation is explosive. Extra care must be taken in these uncertain times.'

Then Barney waved a quick goodbye and climbed into the station wagon.

Elizabeth watched the car speed off. A sense of foreboding settled over her.

CHAPTER 11

She'd slipped back into everyday life when it started: a faint queasiness that was stronger every morning.

On a wintery morning, Elizabeth was making her way to the crèche. It had rained the night before and a veil of mist hovered over the damp earth. The air was fragrant with the smell of dew. Before she reached her destination, the sun appeared from behind the clouds, dissipating the mist, and a rainbow arched across the sky. Standing beneath the rainbow, she felt nausea rise in her threatening to overwhelm her, and she leaned against a tree trunk for support. Her thoughts were in chaos. In the flutter of a second, she knew with certainty that she was carrying Robert's child. A smile broke inside her. Taking a deep breath to quell the nausea, she spread her arms out and lifted her face to the warmth of the sun. The knowledge suffused her with joy.

Then she continued walking calmly, with her arms wrapped protectively around her belly, until she greeted the children who were waiting for her. She grasped that this was a turning point in her life.

Elizabeth stood in front of Doctor Joe Marcus. Her feet on the wooden floor were bare, the thin white clinic gown hung loosely on her slight frame.

Doctor Marcus was known to the townsfolk simply as Doc Joe. He had served the community with a deep devotion for many years and was well acquainted with his patients and their extended families. He'd known Elizabeth since birth, the longed-for daughter of Miemie and Karel Apollos, a lively toddler who had grown to fulfill her promise of beauty.

It was the end of another long day. The fine lines around his eyes had deepened and his shoulders were beginning to sag. He smiled kindly at Elizabeth. 'Your baby should be born about Christmas day.' He waggled his wrist slowly, fingers splayed to emphasise 'about'.

At his words, Elizabeth could hear her heartbeat, and feel the rapid flicker of her pulse. The room smelled of soap and Dettol.

With a sweeping gesture, Doc Joe offered her a seat at his desk and she sat facing him. She saw anxiety reflected in his eyes. He rubbed his temples with a circular motion. He'd heard the rumours, had heard folk in the waiting room whisper about the Apollos girl and the Englishman.

Unflinching, he gazed into Elizabeth's intelligent green eyes. 'It's not too late Elizabeth. If you don't want . . .' his voice trailed off.

'But I do, Doc Joe. I want this child. Robert and I love each other and plan to marry as soon as he gets back to Tweefontein from London.' Her jaw was set resolutely.

Doc Joe put a hand to his forehead, shading his eyes lest Elizabeth see what troubled him. 'Well then, Libby, I'll see you next month. Meanwhile, get enough rest.' Before she left, he put an arm protectively across her shoulders and gave her a quick hug. 'Visit me anytime you need. I'm always pleased to see you.'

There was a pocket of quiet inside Elizabeth as she warmed herself in the wintery sunshine once she'd left the clinic. She walked towards a familiar children's playground that was situated close to the clinic. The sound of laughter rang out in the late afternoon air. Mothers were pushing strollers, while others followed behind their active toddlers. 'Higher, higher,' a child called as a swing arched into the sky. Much of her childhood had been spent at the playground. She settled on a bench under a tree. Hugging her arms around her chest, she absorbed the magnitude of Doc Joe's words. Her thoughts turned to Robert. She would send him a message by contacting the emergency number that Barney had given her. Her troubled reverie included Miemie and Karel. The contentedness and predictability of their lives were about to change. How would they adapt to their unmarried daughter's pregnancy? A chill passed down her spine at the thought of telling them.

And then there was Freda Coetzee – Tannie Freda.

By the time her swirling thoughts had settled, she had made a decision.

CHAPTER 12

Soon after Dirk Coetzee brought his young bride Freda to live in the stately old homestead on Tweefontein, Miemie was employed to work as a housemaid. Many generations of Coetzees had lived in the farmhouse while they tilled the soil and produced acclaimed vintage wines.

Freda and Miemie, both newly married, had bonded and shared experiences of raising their babies. It was a lasting friendship and would carry them through all the vicissitudes of their lives.

The Coetzee children, Helene and Dirk Junior, were close playmates of Elizabeth's. They grew up together, racing around the farm, petting the animals, and splashing in the river until both Coetzee children were sent to boarding school in the city. Elizabeth looked forward to the school breaks when they returned and could resume their carefree games.

She had spent much of her childhood in the Coetzee's home and Freda had a motherly affection for Miemie's daughter.

Freda had become aware of the meetings being held on the farm and, although it disturbed her, she had chosen to turn a blind eye.

Elizabeth knew with certainty that she could confide in Tannie Freda.

The pattern of red roses on the worn, softly upholstered armchair had faded, but the chair still stood in the corner of the farmhouse kitchen, close to the stove, where it had been ever since Elizabeth was a toddler. Now she was curled up on it, her legs tucked beneath her.

It brought her back to a simpler time when, as a child, she had spent hours in the chair, talking to her doll and brushing its hair while Ma peeled the potatoes, carrots and onions picked from the farm garden. Tannie Freda would fill large glass vases with white lilies that grew abundantly on the farm. Then, as now, the warmth emanating from the wood-burning kitchen range created a safe and trusted space for Elizabeth.

Tannie Freda sat on a high-backed kitchen chair beside her, their heads bent together. Freda was absorbed in Elizabeth's story. Alternately, she twisted her wedding ring and touched her throat, while her light-blue eyes were fixed on Elizabeth. She listened with patience, her face full of wisdom. After a long and thoughtful pause, she spoke to Elizabeth, choosing her words carefully.

'Libby, your parents must be told. Miemie is a strong woman. She and Karel will always support you.' She leaned back with her hands folded in her lap, gazing into the distance. 'They always wanted another child. I'm sure they'll embrace a grandchild once they accept your situation.' Reaching out, she took Elizabeth's hands into her own. 'Robert needs to be here to support you and must be told immediately.' She locked eyes with the girl, 'You know, of course, that you can always depend on Dirk and me.'

Elizabeth lowered her head, murmuring a tearful 'thank you' and rose to leave. 'I must hurry home while it is still light.'

'Before you leave,' said Freda, 'take one of the koeksisters that we baked this morning. I know they're your favourite treat.' She lifted the dish containing the syrupy confectionery off the kitchen table. 'Oh, you'd better take another one.' Then she smiled broadly, 'That one is for our baby.'

The evening air felt good on her skin as Elizabeth strode towards home. The promise of spring was in the light breeze. Visiting Tannie Freda bestowed her with a feeling of calm.

But she was unprepared for the wail that would spring from Miemie's throat when she broke the news to her.

She arrived at the cottage to find Karel and Miemie seated at the kitchen table. Candlelight licked the walls . . . the tempting smell of Miemie's cooking filled her nostrils . . . the newspaper rustled in Karel's hands as he turned the pages of *The Cape Argus*.

She kissed both of her parents on their foreheads and took a seat alongside them.

Miemie piled Elizabeth's plate with crisp roast chicken, cinnamon pumpkin and sweet potatoes. Karel put down the paper and crossed his arms across his chest. He gazed enquiringly at her through narrowed eyes. It unsettled Elizabeth. Her Pa, the keeper of her secrets and the weaver of her dreams, seemed to sense that something was amiss.

She could hold back no longer. With all the courage she could muster, she looked steadily at Karel and relayed Doctor Joe's report.

Karel froze and dropped the utensils he'd been holding. They clattered loudly onto the plate.

Miemie emitted a wail and her hands flew to her head as she rocked from side to side.

The air in the room became oppressively warm.

Hours later, when the candles had burned low, the three were still seated around the table, slowly coming to terms with the unexpected turn their lives had taken and the implications of a racially mixed relationship.

Pa, had managed to restore calm. 'It will be all right,' he soothed and turned to face Miemie. Addressing both Miemie and Elizabeth, he said, 'When Robert arrives, he'll marry Libby and the Apollo's will have a beautiful grandchild.' He clapped his hands for emphasis.

His words were part conviction, mostly prayer.

CHAPTER 13

LONDON

The strident ring of the telephone cut across the clatter coming from the typists' pool. Robert strode purposefully towards it, lifting the receiver from its cradle. 'Good day. Robert Booth, speaking.' Upon hearing the voice at the other end, his eyes lit up and his face was wreathed in smiles. 'So good to hear from you, David. I trust you have arrived safely in London?'

Robert listened attentively to David's account of leaving South Africa. Then he glanced at his wristwatch. 'My friend, I'm sorry to cut you short but I am due in court within the hour. Meet me at the Asian restaurant on the bank of the Thames across the Putney Bridge, the same one we lunched at last year. Is six o'clock good for you?'

Checking his briefcase, Robert called instructions to his secretary over his shoulder as he hurried out of the building.

The summer's day was uncomfortably warm and beads of perspiration trickled down his forehead. He wiped an arm across his brow and hailed a taxi. Gratefully, he sank onto the leather seat in the air-conditioned interior.

At the restaurant, a slight breeze coming off the river cooled the air. David stretched his legs in front of him and loosened the top button of his shirt, running a finger inside the damp collar.

He was waiting for Robert.

He didn't have long to wait.

The two men embraced, shaking hands the African way by first clasping thumbs.

David beckoned to the waiter who placed cold beers on the table. Leaning back in his seat, Robert grinned. 'It's good to see you. Now tell me how you managed to get out of South Africa.'

The next few hours sped by as the men exchanged stories. David related how he'd managed to cross the border successfully into Swaziland by masquerading as a businessman. Soon his wife and daughters followed him into exile in London.

Robert needed a partner in his rapidly growing law practice. They agreed that David would fulfill that function, while both men continued to work tirelessly for a group that funded the underground movement in South Africa.

David's jaw clenched and he looked into the distance. When he spoke, there was a hard edge to his voice. He spoke of the suffering and deprivation of living in exile. Then David shrugged his shoulders nonchalantly. 'I don't doubt it'll eventually be worth all the hardships and that soon we'll live in peace in a free South Africa.' He leaned back, playfully jabbing an index finger at Robert. 'So, what's all this talk I'm hearing about you and the Apollos girl?'

Sheepishly, Robert looked away, but when he turned to face David, there was a determined look in his eyes. I love her and intend to bring her to London and marry her. I know how devoted she is to her family and eventually we'll return to Cape Town, which is one of the most beautiful cities in the world.' He paused, as though searching for the right words, then added, 'Its beauty is a deceptive façade – I sense a sinister underbelly.'

'Be careful, Rob,' said David. A serious expression replaced his previous jocularity. 'There have been recent arrests, our leaders imprisoned. I was fortunate to escape. Elizabeth has been kept under the radar until now. She's a good girl, please don't put her in harm's way.'

'I'm aware. I'm following instructions from headquarters that prevent me to make contact with her yet.'

The late evening sun had begun to set when the two men parted, each setting off to their respective homes.

When Robert arrived at his office the following morning, a faxed message from Elizabeth was lying on his desk. It was relayed to him from Barney Stern and contained only two words:

I'm pregnant.

Robert read, then reread, the stark words in the message. His hands trembled. The room seemed to tilt and he steadied himself on the edge of his desk. Sinking into a nearby chair, he buried his head in his hands. It felt as though his world had shifted on its axis, but a thread connected him to reality. He had to find a way of getting back to South Africa – most importantly, back to Elizabeth.

He got up and opened the cabinet in the corner of his office where he kept a bottle of whisky for special occasions and important clients. He splashed a measure into a tumbler, took a steadying gulp, and then settled behind his desk.

He called for his secretary, Claire Mullins, who'd been his trusted assistant for the past year. In her fashionable Soho outfits and beehive hairstyle, she'd proven to be an efficient typist. Her red nails flew across the keyboard, delivering important papers. Robert had come to depend on her, and she had never let him down.

The click of her stilettos came to an abrupt halt after entering the office. Her eyes widened in disbelief. The sight of her impeccable boss with his tie askew and an alcoholic drink in hand, in the morning, caused her jaw to drop.

Abashed, Robert smiled lopsidedly at her, beckoning her to come in. She sat at the desk, facing him.

He studied her carefully before he spoke. 'Miss Mullins, I have an assignment for you. Please call a taxi and deliver this envelope in person to the address on the front. Hand it to the doorman. Do not wait for a reply but come straight back to the office.'

Claire Mullins was perplexed, but at typing college she'd been trained never to ask questions.

Robert waited for a call from headquarters in response to his request that Claire Mullins had delivered. He jumped nervously at every ring from the switchboard.

It was the end of the working day and he was alone in his office. A thrumming silence had replaced the clatter of typewriters. He was absentmindedly going through the briefs on his desk when the call came.

The voice on the other end was gruff, the message short and to the point. 'You cannot go to South Africa. It is too dangerous. Protest action against the Afrikaans language that started in Soweto has quickly spread throughout the country. Any suspicious person is imprisoned without trial. Our intelligence has sent information that Elizabeth Apollos has become of special interest to the security police. Have no contact with her. If you are concerned for her safety, stay away from her. Do not send messages. South Africa is a ticking time bomb. We will advise you when there is a safe corridor to travel.'

Then the line was cut.

Robert held the humming receiver for a moment and then, feeling helpless, dropped it into its cradle. He had no choice but to heed the instructions from Head Office. There could be no contact with Elizabeth. Despondently, he headed out of the office for home.

Lost in a punishing reverie, he had not noticed the open bottle of whisky he'd left standing on his desk.

CHAPTER 14

TWEEFONTEIN

At Tweefontein, the promise of spring had slipped into the chill of winter. Tiny green shoots appeared on the gnarled vines and the scent of apple blossom permeated the air. Tulips transformed the farm's garden into a carpet of vibrant colour.

In the homestead kitchen, the blue gingham curtains were drawn back across the windows. Morning sun flooded the room, bathing Elizabeth in an amber glow and burnished her hair to a deep mahogany. She shifted uncomfortably in the armchair with her arms folded across her swollen belly, her eyes downcast.

There had been no word from Robert. Endless days filled with longing for him had slipped by and Elizabeth's hopes that he'd come back had faded. She accepted that she would care for their child without him. The pitying glances from Ma and Pa, as well as from the other farmworkers, caused her to descend into an abyss of melancholy.

Freda stood with her back to Elizabeth. She sensed Elizabeth's despair, but hummed as she stirred a pot of thick lentil soup that bubbled on the stove. Filling a mug with the steaming liquid, she handed it to Elizabeth who inhaled its aroma and wrapped her hands around the mug, lifting it to her lips. Her eyes, dark pools of despondency, looked into Freda's.

With her hands on her hips, Freda stepped back and raised her eyebrows. 'Still no news from Robert?'

'He has deserted me. Broken his promise.' Elizabeth's lips quivered. 'Now that he's back in London he's forgotten about me.' Her voice was mournful. 'All my efforts to contact Barney have come to nothing. It seems that the emergency number he gave me to call has been disconnected.'

Freda's heart twisted. 'There now,' she said soothingly and, trying to sound positive, added, 'Don't give up hope yet. There are still weeks to go before the baby is born and Robert is sure to contact you when he can. Besides, your Ma and Pa will always support you. So will all of us on Tweefontein. The arrival of a baby is a special event.'

Freda bent over and cradled Elizabeth in her arms, rocking her gently as though she were still a child.

Only then did tears flow; Elizabeth sobbed in Freda's arms, her sobs the heart-rending sounds of abandoned hope.

A deep furrow creased Doc Joe's brow and his eyes squinted in concentration. Then he looked up smiling triumphantly. 'Hear that,' he said, handing his stethoscope to Elizabeth who lay on the examination table.

Thump . . . thump . . . thump, the sound reverberated through the stethoscope into her ears.

'That's your baby's heartbeat,' said Doc Joe beaming with pride.

Elizabeth grasped his hand; her eyes were glistening with tears. 'Will it be soon?'

'Your baby should be born anytime now. Be prepared. You have the instructions I gave you.' He patted her arm reassuringly and squeezed her hand. Then he raised his eyebrows and cocked his head, the question silent on his lips.

'I've had no word from Robert,' she said, lowering her eyelids.

Back in the farmhouse kitchen, Miemie and Katie Plaatjies were preparing for a dinner party that Dirk and Freda were hosting in the formal dining room that evening.

Freda had chosen the wine and was at the kitchen sink arranging hydrangeas in crystal vases. Katie and Miemie faced each other on opposite sides of the kitchen table. Armed with a rolling pin, Katie was vigorously rolling pastry on a wooden board, her plump arms shaking with the exertion. She held the flattened sheet up with both hands and considered its lightness. Satisfied, she pressed it into the bottom of a dish. She was proud of her pies, the most sought-after in the district. She wiped her brow with the back of her hand and then, putting both hands on her ample hips, looked shrewdly at Miemie. 'Will the Englishman be here for the birth of Elizabeth's baby?'

Miemie felt her insides lurch, but answered defiantly, 'I'm sure he will. He loves my Libby.'

'The talk among the farmworkers is that he has abandoned your girl,' Katie said, nodding knowingly.

'That's not true. They are *skinderbeks*, gossipmongers,' answered Miemie, her frustration evident in the colour flooding her cheeks. Although she'd begin each day filled with hope, it always ended in disappointment. Still, she clung to her belief that Robert would return.

Freda, overhearing the conversation, intervened exuding calm. 'Katie, whether Robert returns or not, we will all support Elizabeth and the baby.'

For Miemie it was the final acceptance of her disappointment. She buried her face in her apron and wept.

It was a balmy midsummer evening, the sky a carpet of stars. The air felt magical.

All day the sun had beaten down on the valley, causing the residents of Tweefontein to seek refuge from the heat under the giant willow tree down at the river. The children's lithe brown bodies glistened with droplets of water and farm dogs lapped at the water's edge, grateful for respite from the blistering heat.

In the Apollos home, doors and windows had been thrown wide open to encourage a cooling breeze to pass through and temper the enervating heat. Elizabeth, heavily pregnant, sprawled uncomfortably on the couch. Miemie and Karel fussed about, attempting to relieve her discomfort.

Television had recently been introduced into South Africa and the black-and-white set stood proudly where once the transistor radio had been. The announcer's voice filled the room, while mesmerising scenes were enacted on the screen. A bomb exploded on a railway line . . . a police station was attacked resulting in civilian casualties . . . John Vorster emerged victorious from the recent general election.

Elizabeth felt a familiar shudder down her spine. It was all happening as Barney had predicted. His connections with the underground kept him informed of insurgents and her heart contracted with fear for both his and Robert's safety.

Just then, the first contraction struck. Elizabeth gasped with the pain. And again, with the following one. She was consumed with both excitement and fear. Following Doc Joe's instructions, she calmly informed Miemie and Karel that the baby's birth was imminent.

They sprang into action. Karel ran most of the way to the farmhouse. Stumbling up to the front veranda and breathing heavily from the exertion, he knocked frantically at the door. It was opened swiftly by Dirk. Between gulps of air, Karel relayed his message.

Within minutes Elizabeth was bundled into Dirk's old Mercedes for the short ride to the hospital. A message had been sent to Doc Joe who was waiting expectantly.

In the hospital waiting room, time passed tediously for Miemie and Karel. The wall clock ticked away the hours loudly in the silence. Through the long night, their eyelids drooped but they jerked open with any sudden movement or the sound of a passer-by.

The horizon was silvering when a baby's lusty wail broke the stillness of the morning.

Rubbing the sleep from their eyes, Miemie and Karel Apollos stumbled towards a haggard Doc Joe, who cradled a blanketed bundle in his arms. 'Meet your granddaughter,' he said, with a broad smile. 'Elizabeth is safely delivered of a healthy daughter. Congratulations.'

Miemie was the first to draw back the blanket and gaze in awe at the tiny face beneath. She gasped, her eyes widening. Swaying slightly, she grasped Karel's arm.

'Karel,' she barely whispered, '*Die kind is wit* – the child is white.'

CHAPTER 15

LONDON

Steel-grey clouds blanketed the sky in London, leaving the world monochrome. In the murky light of day's end, pearls of frost glistened on bare branches. There had been a snow warning that morning.

Robert wound a woollen scarf around his neck and, hunching his shoulders into his fleece-lined coat, got ready to leave his office. He gazed through the window. The desolate scene matched his mood. For the past weeks, all his thoughts centred on Elizabeth and the imminent birth of their child. Helplessness at not being able to communicate with her had left him gloomy and depressed.

Peering through the window and lost in thought, he found himself explaining to Elizabeth in his mind why he couldn't reach her in South Africa. 'Please forgive me,' he said aloud. He'd find himself in mental conversation with her many times a day.

He fumbled with the keys outside the door and was about to lock it when he was alerted to the ring of the fax machine. *Can it wait until tomorrow?* He frowned, deliberating. Then, on instinct, he retraced his steps back into the office and withdrew the page from the fax machine.

There it was: Elizabeth Apollos was safely delivered of a healthy daughter at six o'clock this morning.

All the colour drained from Robert's face. Unsteadily, he eased himself into a chair, his thoughts in disarray

Time passed while he absorbed the magnitude of the message. When he'd recovered his composure, he made an irreversible decision.

There was a determined set to his jaw when he finally locked the office door.

His breath turned to fog in the crisp evening air. A taxi cruised past, its headlights splintering the mist into a prism of colour. He hailed it and, through the open window, gave the driver the address.

An impossible ache gnawed at him as he stood on the doorstep of an old semi-detached house. He lifted the heavy metal knocker and heard its blows reverberate, and then the tread of footsteps down the passage.

The front door was flung open. David Moses stood framed in the doorway with three of his littlest children clinging to his legs, their eyes dancing with curiosity. David looked at him in surprise. 'Do come inside Robert. What brings you here in this freezing weather?'

Pleased by the warmth of coals glowing in the open hearth, Robert embraced David and patted the heads of the children who gazed solemnly up at him. 'I need to speak to you. Something urgent has come about,' he said, before settling into an armchair in front of the hearth.

David poured each a measure of whisky and eased into a seat facing Robert. The light from the coals bathed the room in an amber glow.

David leaned forward. 'My friend, what troubles you?'

'My daughter was born this morning.'

A smile broke across David's face. 'Congratulations!' he said, standing up to clink his glass against Robert's.

The ticking mantelpiece clock recorded the minutes as Robert informed his friend of his need to get back to South Africa and to reach Elizabeth and his daughter. He looked steadily at David, the firelight reflecting the anxiety in his eyes. 'I don't wish to put Elizabeth or myself in any danger, but I need your help to get to South Africa.'

David steepled his hands beneath his chin for a few thoughtful minutes before he answered. 'The Soweto riots have plunged South Africa into instability,' he said, solemnly. 'Those of us living here in exile, myself included, are calling for international intervention and sanctions. It's dangerous for you to be in South Africa. However,' he sighed deeply, 'if you're determined to be with Elizabeth, I'll try to help you. But be mindful of the implications. A meeting is being held tomorrow and I'll discuss your situation. Someone will get back to you by the end of the day.'

The tense atmosphere lightened when Anna, David's wife, entered carrying two bowls of steaming soup. After handing one to each man, she hugged Robert warmly. 'This is bean soup,' she said. 'The way we make it back home.'

Robert devoured the soup, surprised by how hungry he was. Cocooned in the warmth of Anna and David's friendship, he felt his tension ease. Time passed while he related his story to Anna. She was riveted and made little clicking sounds of sympathy as she absorbed the details of his dilemma.

'Has it been difficult for you to settle in London after leaving South Africa?' Robert ventured.

She lowered her head and was quiet for a moment. When she looked up, he saw the pain in her eyes. 'We left our families and dear friends behind in Malansdorp and, in our hurry to leave, we never got to say goodbye. But we knew we were in danger and faced imprisonment if we stayed. We have settled here though it'll never be home, and we don't know when we'll return or what we'll find there when we do. But,' she added, brightening up, 'we have the support of other exiled families living here.'

Robert glanced at the mantelpiece clock, alarmed by how much time had elapsed. Thanking them hurriedly, he prepared to leave. Once settled in the taxi on his way home, he spoke again to Elizabeth in his mind.

'Not long now. Soon the three of us will be together.'

Robert paced his office impatiently, waiting for the call that David had promised. When, at last, it came, he cradled the receiver beneath his chin and listened intently.

There was no mistaking the gravity of David's voice. 'It has been agreed that, given the circumstances, you'll be provided with a passport and documents to assist you to reach South Africa. You'll go under an assumed name.'

When it came, the warning was clear: 'You're embarking on a dangerous journey and we cannot guarantee your safety. Good luck, my friend,' David said, and then he cut the line.

CHAPTER 16

TWEEFONTEIN
31st DECEMBER, 1978

To herald the new year, Dirk and Freda hosted Tweefontein's annual New Year's Eve party to show their appreciation for the workers. It was a tradition established by the Elder Coetzees and perpetuated by following generations.

The enticing smell from the barbeque filled the air. Flames licked the coals in the half barrels on which coils of boerewors and lamb chops sizzled. Paper plates were refilled many times.

A dazzling firework display was held; fluorescent stars and streamers streaked across the night sky forming rainbows of colour. Enthralled, everyone gazed in awe, pointing to a golden shower of stars pouring down from the heavens. The music of Clout and Abba drifted from gramophones, and young and old danced to the tunes of 'Substitute' and 'Thank you for the music'. Tickeydraai, a traditional South African dance, was enjoyed with gusto.

Three-week-old baby Emmy lay sleeping peacefully in her mother's arms, oblivious of the festivities all around her. Elizabeth had joined a group who fussed over the baby, passing her around the circle of arms. She enjoyed the camaraderie of her friends who had rallied around her since Emmy's birth.

Miemie watched her surreptitiously from across the way. 'Karel,' she said while clapping her hands in time to the music, 'our child seems so happy tonight. See how she's smiling.'

Contentment shone on Miemie's face. She'd washed and ironed her best Sunday dress to wear to this party – the green one with the ruffled white collar and shiny buttons down the back – and had pinned back her curly grey hair with a green slide to match her dress. She delighted in the relaxed atmosphere after the strain of the past few months.

'Dance with me,' she said, and pulled a reluctant Karel towards a group swaying to the music under a star-speckled sky.

Karel circled Miemie's waist with his arms while she nestled her head on his chest. He danced with his Miemie, his first and only love. But his heart was heavy. Although Elizabeth seemed happy, he knew that there was a wounded place deep within her, a place that he could never reach. He saw the pain reflected in her eyes. The memory of Robert Booth was slowly receding from their lives and, they'd come to accept that he would not return to Elizabeth and his child.

The challenges of raising a white child in their coloured community still loomed large in their lives. Although Dirk Coetzee was a staunch card-carrying member of the Nationalist Party, he was fond of the Apollos family and had decided to protect them against probing enquiries related to the politics of the day.

Katie Plaatjies wiped her hands on her coal-smeared apron and placed the long-handled fork, which she had used to turn over the boerewors, on the table beside the barrel with its smoldering coals. Katie walked over to Elizabeth who was among her circle of friends.

'Ah, do let me see the baby,' she crooned, giving Elizabeth a motherly smile. She peered down at Emmy who was cocooned in a pink knitted shawl. Then her eyes widened and she stepped backward. 'She's white,' she gasped and placed her hand over her mouth. Her face softened. 'Ag shame, Libby,' she said soothingly. 'She's still young. Her skin will turn brown as she grows older.' Nodding sagely, she walked away.

Somewhere in the distance, a clock struck.

A chorus of voices rose, 'Five, four, three . . .'

Another burst of gold and silver stars lit up the sky.

It was 1978.

CHAPTER 17

Weeks had passed since the call from David that granted Robert permission to fly to Cape Town. He'd waited anxiously for the arrival of a passport and documents. The waiting seemed endless. Then two days ago David had appeared in his office carrying a large Manila envelope. He brushed the snow off the shoulders of his woollen coat and removed his knitted beanie, and dropped into the chair beside the desk. He cocked his head, 'Is this what you're waiting for?' passing the envelope across the desk to Robert's outstretched hand.

Robert's drawn features revealed his apprehension.

David shrewdly anticipated Robert's concern, 'I'll take care of the practice while you're away. You'll have no reason to worry.' He shrugged and turned his palms up.

A weight lifted visibly off Robert's shoulders, and he smiled wanly.

Robert shifted with the motion of the plane as it lurched in the turbulent African sky. His long, slim fingers curled around a coffee cup, steadying it on the tray in front of him. The hostess had smiled indulgently when she handed him the last coffee, the one that he now held steady. He had consumed endless cups of it to keep alert. Catching sight of his reflection in the plane's window, he noted that his eyes were those of a man who had not slept. The cabin was quiet except for the low hum of the engine.

They were about to land in Cape Town. The wheels hit the runway and the plane shuddered as it thundered onwards before slowly coming to a halt. Soon he would have to pass through customs. Panic caused a bitter taste to rise in his throat, and he swallowed a mouthful of the tepid coffee.

His thoughts turned to Elizabeth. No message had been forwarded to alert her of his return. His emotions churned. He took a pen out of his pocket and clicked it nervously as the plane taxied on the tarmac towards waiting buses. At the customs desk, the official glanced briefly at his passport, stamped it and waved him through. 'Enjoy your stay with us, Mister Martin.'

He stepped out of the airport into the warmth of the African sun. His shoulders sagged with relief. Barney was waiting for him.

He steered Robert towards a parked car. Within minutes, they were on their way to Tweefontein.

Sun streamed through the window pooling around Elizabeth. She sat in a rocking chair cradling Emmy. Although it was only mid-morning, the heat had intensified causing the baby to become fretful. Elizabeth rocked her gently, crooning childhood lullabies. She heard the shudder of a car's engine come to a halt outside the cottage. The slam of heavy doors was followed by an urgent banging on the front door.

She froze, clutching Emmy protectively to her.

The fear of a visit by the apartheid police, the Special Unit, terrified her. She knew it could take one accidental whisper to the wrong person for this to happen.

Miemie opened the front door and stifled a scream.

Elizabeth's stomach clenched and the blood drained from her face.

Then she looked up.

He was silhouetted in the doorway against the bright morning sun. Her vision blurred. Cautiously, he walked towards her, his arms outstretched. As he came closer, the dark outline bloomed into colour and filled out into the form of Robert Booth and she knew that this moment would be imprinted in her memory forever.

He knelt beside the rocking chair, circling Elizabeth and Emmy in his arms. The toll of months of anxiety was etched into his drawn features. She touched his cheek. She remembered all the conversations she had dreamed of having with him; now all words died on her lips, left unspoken.

He stroked Emmy's soft hand and his baby's little fingers gripped his. He saw Elizabeth's gentle features and his own penetrating blue eyes in his daughter's face and the stirrings of a new emotion rose in his chest.

Barney watched the scene as it was being enacted. Delight lit up his ruddy features.

Karel and Miemie were confused by the sudden development.

Miemie bustled about the kitchen, steadying her nerves by preparing a meal. She covered the table with a red checked cloth and set out the cutlery. Soon a pot of soup simmered on the coal stove, the rich aroma filling the room.

Barney drew Karel out of earshot. In measured tones, he described the events leading up to Robert's unexpected arrival. Karel's distress heightened. He was aware of the danger that Robert's visit presented. He feared the apartheid police. Stories had filtered through to him of the government's increased brutality as they fought against the inevitability of a regime change. He understood the fragility of his world.

Behind a closed door, the voices of Elizabeth and Robert droned on, sometimes softly, mostly raised; the anger of Elizabeth, the frustration of Robert. Karel, Miemie and Barney's eyes darted anxiously towards the door. Finally, the door opened and the couple emerged, contentedly holding hands.

No one asked about the raised voices.

They gathered around the lunch table in the kitchen and sat down to eat in the warm glow of their momentary happiness, still untouched by what their future held.

As the hours passed, the news of Robert's arrival spread quickly.

Groups congregated, whispering behind their hands. 'The Englishman is back,' they said in astonishment, inventing reasons for his return.

Inside the cottage, the atmosphere was euphoric.

Robert had an energy that filled the room and the sorrow that had burdened Elizabeth lifted. She clung to the feeling of happiness.

On the hob, the kettle sang and again the best porcelain tea set was on the kitchen table. The news had reached the farmhouse and Katie delivered a batch of crisp, syrupy koeksisters for the celebration.

All the while, largely unnoticed, the television played in the background. Images flashed on the screen of the South African Defence Force attacking Swapo bases in Angola. The Nationalist Government had tried to keep television out of South Africa, considering it a threat to its hold on power, but had finally relented. Now inevitable change caused instability and the atmosphere in the country was explosive.

As evening approached, Robert made his way to the homestead to meet Dirk, who had been waiting for him and watched him stride along the path towards the front stoep.

Although a long-standing member of the Broederbond, Dirk felt a growing unease about the progressively harsher laws inflicted on the black community. He was unsettled. The violence and mayhem exploding in his country on both sides of the political spectrum was not his vision for the land he loved. During long sleepless nights, he paced on the creaking wooden floorboards of the farmhouse, questioning his beliefs. The arrival of baby Emmy, of whom he was growing ever fonder, cast a light on the plight of innocent people who were caught up in unlawful and unjust situations only because of their skin colour.

Guilt gnawed at him. Gradually, he was beginning to admire the courageous men and women who fought a treacherous system that would ultimately benefit no one.

'Welcome friend,' he said and extended his hand to Robert. 'I've been expecting you. There are serious matters we need to discuss.'

Soon an open bottle of Tweefontein wine, glittering like garnets, rested on the table between the two men seated on the stoep, where the shade of great oak trees eased the torrid heat. Immersed in conversation, their heads were bent close together.

The rays of the sun were lowering while Dirk relayed grave details of the current situation in South Africa, emphasising the challenges of interracial relationships and raising a finger to make a point. It hardened Robert's resolve to leave Tweefontien the following morning, taking Elizabeth and Emmy with him.

The wine bottle was empty by the time he squinted at his wristwatch and rose to leave. Dirk threw a friendly arm around Robert's shoulders, but there was no mistaking the solemn stance of both men.

The sky had dimmed when Robert reached the cottage. Barney had left for the city and calmness had been restored. Emmy was asleep in the cradle that Karel had long ago fashioned out of Oregon pine for his daughter. The room was peaceful.

Robert took Elizabeth's hand and led her outside. They walked into the rapidly fading twilight; neither wanting to speak, neither wanting to break the spell. Finally, he turned to Elizabeth, the light of the rising moon illuminating the contours of his face and the determined set of his jaw. He broke the silence. Speaking urgently, he outlined the plan for their escape that Barney had presented to him on the drive out from the airport.

'Elizabeth, when we leave Tweefontein tomorrow morning and go to a safe house in the city, the tranquillity of your country life will change. In London, we'll live peacefully as a family. I don't expect the transition will be easy but I'll be there to support you.'

Elizabeth looked into his eyes and saw his soul. She tightened her grip on his hand and surrendered her future to him.

The night was filled with infinite possibilities.

Elizabeth woke to familiar predawn sounds. In the distance, a rooster heralded the start of a new day. On the edge of the horizon, a rosy glow appeared, and she watched the day gather around her.

She heard the shuffle of footsteps outside the bedroom window and the voices of the workers calling out in greeting. She breathed in the morning air, fully aware that all she found familiar was about to change. Trying to swallow the knot in her throat, she gazed out of the window at the fields of Tweefontein. This was the only home she had ever known.

Barney would soon collect them for the ride into the city.

Miemie and Karel bustled about the tiny kitchen preparing breakfast. The smell of freshly baked bread wafted from the oven. The painful knowledge that Elizabeth and Emmy were leaving, and the uncertainty of their return, drew them close. Yet they clung to the belief that a change of government would soon bring their family together again.

The crunch of tyres at the gate announced Barney's arrival. It jolted Elizabeth, making her confront the finality of her decision and the reality of abandoning her parents to live in a land so far away and about which she knew little. Tears of sorrow and guilt welled up in her eyes, but there was no turning back. She had to draw on her courage and face an uncertain future in a strange country. But she had placed her faith in Robert and didn't regret it.

Miemie stood in the doorway and watched Elizabeth, Emmy and Robert leave with Barney. Anguish stained her face. She wrung her hands and fidgeted with the edge of her apron. Sorrow weighed heavily on her. Before turning away, she lifted her shoulders in a helpless gesture, her palms upturned.

Elizabeth placed her cheek, wet with tears, against Karel's weathered one; unspoken words swirled in the silence between them. Barney called, drawing her away. Reluctantly, Karel forever her north star, walked to the car holding Elizabeth's hand. Before she climbed in, Barney handed her a parcel. Elizabeth raised her eyebrows.

'It's a nurse's uniform,' Barney said. 'I'm afraid you'll have to wear this and sit on the back seat holding Emmy until we reach the safe house in Devil's Peak. Until we get there, you are the nurse to Robert's child.' Barney shuffled his feet in embarrassment, his eyes downcast, and then he gazed directly at her. 'Let's hope this is the last indignity you'll suffer in South Africa, your own country, before the laws change.'

Seated in Barney's station wagon, Elizabeth twisted around as it picked up speed to watch the receding figures of Ma and Pa, their arms entwined. Their images grew ever smaller until they could no longer be seen.

The workers of Tweefontein had congregated at the gate to bid farewell to their friend. When the car slowed down to pass through the gate, their doleful expressions reflected the loss and sadness they felt on the departure of Elizabeth and more so of Emmy, the baby they'd grown to love.

CHAPTER 18

The house on the slopes of Devil's Peak was indistinguishable from the others that lined Magnolia Street, except out front it had a spacious stoep with a corrugated roof supported by ornate, cast-iron columns.

On their arrival, Zelda Herman stood on the stoep waiting to greet Barney, Elizabeth and Robert. She glanced briefly at Emmy. Tall and imposing, she wore a dark-grey skirt, a button-up white blouse and sensible brown shoes that all added to her appearance of a strict schoolmistress. Her upright posture, stern demeanour and penetrating eyes made it abundantly clear that her rules would be adhered to.

After the hot, tedious drive from Tweefontein, they were relieved to enter the leafy garden and to sit in wicker chairs on the cool stoep. Zelda had prepared iced drinks and sandwiches and placed them on a low wrought-iron table. It was reassuring to find all the necessities for Emmy piled up alongside.

Later that day, after they had settled down and house rules laid out, they gathered in the high-ceilinged sitting room that closed shutters kept cool and dark. Emmy slept peacefully in a carrycot at her mother's feet, unaware of the simmering tension inside the room.

Zelda sat on a wing-backed chair; her feet planted squarely on the floor. She swivelled her head from side to side as she rested her eyes on each of her guests. 'I've harboured many fleeing activists,' she said. 'None are as wanted by the security police as the three of you are. One wrong move or unintended word will be a death knell for all. Extra precautions must be taken.' She glanced at Elizabeth. 'You'll remain Emmy's nurse for the time that you spend here. I've told my neighbours that my nephew, his baby and a nurse will be staying with me.' Her lips pulled into a thin line. 'I hope you'll get permission to leave for London soon.'

Robert listened intently to Zelda's monologue. His brow furrowed and he exchanged worried glances with Barney, who was about to leave.

'I'll deliver your air tickets for London as soon as I receive them. I've been told that passenger lists are being scrutinised. Be patient. We're waiting for an undercover customs official to be on duty so that we can safely get you through.' He heaved a deep sigh as he headed for the door. 'I hope to be seeing you soon.'

The days crawled by.

Emmy was the catalyst that sealed their friendship with Zelda. She was captivated by the baby. Her expression softened whenever she held Emmy, rocking her gently and drinking in her powdery smell.

Consumed with worry, Robert read the daily newspapers and listened to the overseas news broadcasts on a transistor radio. Being unable to contact David Moses increased his unease.

Days passed and there was still no sign of Barney or the air tickets.

The stifling summer days were cooling down. Zelda had prepared a light supper of boerewors rolls served with pickled relish and had set it out on the stoep. Strongly brewed coffee and melktert rounded off the meal.

They watched the moon as it rose, adrift above Signal Hill. Below them, the lights of Cape Town sparkled like diamonds strewn across black velvet. In the hush of night, as they lingered over the meal, refilling their coffee mugs, they had got to know more about their formidable host, Zelda Herman.

'When did you become involved in the cause,' Robert asked her. He drained his mug and wiped his mouth with the back of his hand.

Zelda drummed her fingers on the arm of the chair and then folded her hands in her lap. Memories softened her voice. 'I was young and impressionable,' she said with a sigh, 'and I was an ambitious journalist working on a newspaper in Johannesburg. My stance opposing the government appeared frequently in published articles, to the politicians' ire. I knew I was being watched, but that didn't daunt me and I continued criticising them. It was an exciting time.'

Robert frowned slightly. 'What brought you to Cape Town?'

'I married a lawyer, Dan Herman, who was an activist. We settled in Cape Town. I resigned from the newspaper and gave up my career to work for the opposition. Dan was arrested by the security police and kept in detention for ninety days. He was never the same. After his release, he was frail and mentally detached and died a year later of a heart attack. We knew that it was the effect of the torture inflicted on him during his imprisonment. His death made me more determined to fight for justice.'

Elizabeth was deeply moved and took Zelda's hand in hers. 'All South Africans are grateful to you for being brave and not giving up.'

Zelda turned enquiringly to Robert.

He shifted in his seat, stretched his long legs in front of him and crossed his ankles. He stared into the distance, sifting through his memory, and then he spoke in a soft, broken voice.

'My mother died when I was eight years old. I was fourteen when I was in a car accident in London. My father was driving. He did not survive. It took three months in the hospital for me to recover. I was an only child and was sent to Cape Town to stay with my aunt and uncle who were childless. They didn't know how to take care of me, but were supportive and helped me through school.'

Robert's jaw clenched. He was silent for a few moments collecting his thoughts before he continued. 'My father had left sufficient funds for my education and, after matriculating, I enrolled at UCT to read law. While there, I began attending rallies and met young people who, like myself, were appalled by this regime's unjust treatment of blacks and coloureds and who were prepared to fight for change. We formed groups and that's when I met Barney Stern. I was part of a group clandestinely printing pamphlets with anti-government slogans. Sipho Bantu was a printer and we became firm friends and stayed in touch after I left Cape Town for London. The net was closing in on me. I left to protect my aunt and uncle against my involvement with the underground. In London, I requalified and set up practice, continuing my work with lobby groups against the apartheid regime.'

Then he rose to refill his mug from the percolator. His eyes were clouded with an emotion that Elizabeth found hard to fathom.

The stars were beginning to fade. A pale light crept in at the edge of the horizon.

In silence, they watched the night slowly dissolve.

Three people whose destinies were entwined witnessing the first light of a new dawn.

An urgent banging at the front door roused Robert from a fitful sleep. He shook his head to clear the confusion and glanced at his wristwatch. The luminous dial glowed in the dark. Two-twenty.

The banging became louder. More urgent.

Distraught with fear, he threw back the bedclothes and rushed from the room, closing the door behind him. Elizabeth, fully awake, came out comforting a wailing Emmy in her arms. Zelda appeared in a nightgown and slippers. She reached the front door before Robert and Elizabeth.

A frantic Sipho stood in the doorway. 'Robert and Elizabeth must leave!' he stammered, pacing in agitation. 'You must leave right now!' Sweat glistened on his dark skin. 'The police are preparing papers for your arrest. You have an hour before they arrive. I'm instructed to remove you immediately. We'll drive to the border. If all goes according to plan, it should take a week to get there, with stopovers in places like Bloemfontein. Should you make it across, you'll be flown out of the country. Please hurry.'

Zelda took control of the situation. After ordering them to dress, she threw their belongings into bags. In the chaos, Elizabeth clutched Emmy protectively to her breast. Sipho looked at her sympathetically. 'You can't take her with you, it's too dangerous. Karel and Miemie will be alerted in the morning and be driven here to fetch her. Please hurry, time is running out.'

Elizabeth's face crumpled. She emitted a thin wail. 'I won't leave without her.'

Robert, taking took hold of Elizabeth's shoulders, turned her firmly towards him.

'Taking her with us will put her in danger. There's no guarantee that we'll reach the border without being arrested. Emmy will be safer with Miemie and Karel. We'll send for her when we reach London.'

Zelda tore Emmy from Elizabeth's arms. 'Go now,' she instructed and prodded them towards the door.

Robert part-carried and part-dragged Elizabeth, who was sobbing uncontrollably, to Sipho's car. As the car sped off, sirens could be heard in the distance, renting the night air.

Zelda had firmly closed and locked the front door but soon opened it again at the persistent ring of the doorbell. The officers gained entry by pushing their way in, forcing Zelda aside. She had removed all traces of Robert and Elizabeth. The police ransacked each room, methodically upturning cupboards and drawers. All they found was a baby sleeping in a cot on its back, its little fists curled on either side of its angelic face, and a protective aunt who glared at them.

Hours later, the police prepared to leave, disappointed that they hadn't found incriminating evidence. The sergeant stabbed a finger at Zelda, his eyes narrowed into slits. 'Don't think that this is the end lady, we'll be back.' He looked over his shoulder ominously as he walked away. 'We're watching you.'

The commotion had awakened Emmy, who cried while Zelda soothed her in her arms.

The child was blissfully unaware that, on the cusp of her young life in the house on Magnolia Street beneath the shadow of Table Mountain, her fate had been sealed.

CHAPTER 19

In the weeks after Robert and Elizabeth's audacious escape, Zelda became increasingly aware that the sergeant's threat was not an idle one and that the authorities were keeping an attentive eye on her, preventing Karel and Miemie from collecting Emmy.

At night, lights flashed through the windows of her home; during the day, she noticed a stationary vehicle with blackened windows parked close by. Disruptive midnight phone calls with heavy breathing at the other end occurred regularly. The authorities were attempting to intimidate her. Although their brutal methods could be terrifying, they were not enough to quell her determination to fight the unjust apartheid laws.

Being childless, Zelda was unprepared for the torrent of emotions that the baby stirred up in her. She rejoiced at each new smile and stroked the downy head while she cradled and fed her. Caring for Emmy added a new dimension to what had been an austere existence. Zelda had come to accept that she'd never have a child of her own, but now that she'd bonded with the infant, handing her to her grandparents was not going to be easy. The thought wrenched her heart.

Weeks passed while Zelda waited for the police to end their surveillance, and for the phone calls to stop. When the car with blackened windows no longer appeared on Magnolia Street, it was time to deliver Emmy to Karel and Miemie as she'd promised Elizabeth.

With Emmy strapped into a car seat at the back, Zelda's Datsun sped along the highway towards Tweefontein. The landscape displayed a palette of autumn colours.

A breeze picked up. There was a chill in the air.

Zelda rolled up the window and glanced in her rear-view mirror to check on Emmy. Her thoughts churned. She was devising a plan for Emmy's future, a future she hoped to be a part of. In a rural community, coloured grandparents raising a white child of mixed parentage was certain to be fraught with challenges. Notions such as these intruded into her sleep at night.

She acknowledged that the arrival of Emmy had brought changes to her life.

Ornately framed paintings of past Coetzees glared dauntingly down at Miemie and Karel in the front room – the *voorkamer* – as they sat awkwardly on high-backed chairs. Their tension was palpable. A cut-glass vase filled with white lilies stood on a polished mahogany table. The afternoon sun glinted through the blinds, casting oblique shadows on the thick Persian carpet.

Dirk and Freda stood out front waiting to greet Zelda and Emmy. The anticipated arrival of Emmy filled them all with both joy and despair. They were painfully aware that the infant would bring changes to their lives.

Karel clasped and unclasped his hands; his breathing was shallow. Miemie leaned against him for support. The crunch of tyres on gravel alerted them to Zelda's arrival. She entered the room, cradling Emmy in her arms. The child was awake and had begun to whimper. Miemie and Zelda locked eyes before Zelda placed the baby in her arms. Emmy's cries became more frantic. Her little hand grasped at the air reaching for the familiarity of Zelda.

All eyes turned to Miemie, who seemed absorbed by the infant. She rocked her, crooning, until Emmy settled. Then Miemie heaved a sigh that seemed to emerge from somewhere deep inside her. At that moment, all her reservations dissolved. The air in the room was charged with emotion, each person wrapped in their thoughts. The rattle of teacups lightened the atmosphere when Freda put a tray on the table and they gathered around it. The conversation centred around Emmy and the future that they envisioned for her.

Then Zelda pushed her cup aside and leaned forward, pressing her palms onto the table. Her eyes darted about. She spoke earnestly, 'I have arranged for Emmy's financial security.' Her eyes softened as she turned to Miemie and Karel and said, falteringly, 'I've grown fond of your grandchild. It seems that our paths were destined to cross.'

Karel glanced at Zelda over the rim of his cup. He, too, spoke hesitantly and voiced his fears. 'The school on Tweefontein accepts only black and coloured children . . .'

Until that moment, Dirk had not participated in the discussion. He'd absorbed the impact of Zelda's disclosure and Karel's misgivings. He sat back in thought, pinching his chin. Then he stood up and addressed Karel. 'Freda and I have discussed this. If you agree, Emmy will be our niece and, when the time comes, will be enrolled in the junior school for white students in town. I'm in a political position to protect her.'

Miemie interjected hesitantly, her lips quivered. 'But if she's your niece, where will she live?'

'She's your grandchild.' Dirk held up both palms. 'She'll live with you and be raised by you and Karel until Robert and Elizabeth return.'

Miemie choked back tears and turned to Karel. He nodded affirmatively and squeezed her arm, then he looked at everyone around the table. 'We're grateful,' he murmured.

There were smiles and handshakes as Karel and Miemie left the farmhouse, carrying Emmy to her new home.

Zelda gazed at their retreating backs and felt an expanding sense of loss. Emmy's absence would leave a void in her life.

When they had left, Dirk alone with Freda, patted his pocket for his glasses and slipped them on. He turned to her, shrugging his shoulders. But his glasses did not conceal the worry lines in the corner of his eyes or the deep furrow between them.

Emmy's appearance on Tweefontein had woven all the threads of their lives into a tapestry.

CHAPTER 20

ESCAPE

It took Robert and Elizabeth weeks to reach the Botswana border. They had travelled stealthily in the early morning hours and hidden in safe houses at every opportunity in an attempt to keep a low profile, hopefully under the police radar.

Each day presented new challenges; each stranger's face brought the prospect of arrest.

In Bloemfontein, they were advised to separate and be ferried in different vehicles that would frequently be changed to confuse the authorities. The plan was for them to be reunited after crossing the border, but there were no guarantees. They were painfully aware of the fragility of their future.

Reluctantly, they agreed to part. An hour before dawn when the sky was still a vault of stars, Robert walked away from Elizabeth. He strode to a car, its engine revving in readiness for the journey.

Staring at him retreating, Elizabeth had a moment of clarity that she had not had before. 'Robert, wait,' she cried out.

Robert was about to climb into the passenger seat but straightened up when she ran towards him.

'Robert, now I know that what we did for our daughter was the best we could do for her.' She spoke quickly in her eagerness to convey her message. 'She'll be safe in Tweefontein with my family, her future will be assured. Our lives are too uncertain to include her at this time.'

'We will soon be reunited.' Robert spoke with conviction, but his features were veiled with sorrow. 'When she is older, she'll get to know how much we love her and the sacrifice we've made in leaving her behind.' He turned away and climbed into the car. The solitary figure of Elizabeth watching as the car drove off was imprinted in his memory.

The night was filled with secrets.

They boarded a chartered plane that had landed in anticipation of their successful crossing. Within hours they arrived in Egypt.

The sleet lay thick on the ground the night Robert and Elizabeth, aboard a BA flight from Egypt, arrived at Heathrow.

After their perilous escape from South Africa, they had finally reached London.

EMMY

It was the milky smell of her that I missed most. That and her warm breath on my skin when she held me close to her chest. Her eyes were filled with smiles when my tiny fingers tangled her long hair.

I missed her and the sound of her voice.

When she was gone, the arms that held me were stiff and unyielding as though uncertain of what to do with me. But they were kind and became gentler as we grew accustomed to each other.

Zelda bathed and fed me and there was comfort in the routine. Her voice became familiar but, unlike Elizabeth, she used it only when it mattered.

Soon the memory of the milky smell and soulful eyes faded.

It was then that the balance of my life was restored.

PART TWO

CHAPTER 21

LONDON

The frail light of a new dawn filters through high windows. Still, the night's shadows linger.

Robert is immersed in the morning newspaper which he holds up, spread in front of him.

Elizabeth rises from the breakfast table. She adjusts the oblique slats of the blind, allowing light to flow into the room. She draws her dressing gown closer. Twisting her hair in the nape of her neck she folds it around her hand and pins it into a knot. When Robert leaves for the courtroom where he is defending a woman from Harare, she will dress for the city.

'Will I ever become accustomed to this dreary weather?' she muses aloud. 'It's five years since we arrived in London but still I long for the warm African sun.'

But Robert remains unresponsive. He is engrossed in the article he is reading. Steam swirls off the coffee in the mug beside him and the buttered toast remains uneaten. She steps around the table and stands behind him. With her hands on his shoulders, she peers down at the newspaper.

'David and Anna, are expecting us for dinner this evening.' Her voice is plaintive, trying to attract his attention.

'Uh huh,' he answers, absentmindedly. Then he punches the paper and grins triumphantly.

'It is beginning to happen, Libby,' his breath catches with excitement. 'The South African Government is becoming desperate. They're imposing laws that will surely split the party. A more militant culture is emerging and important new organisations are being formed. It won't be long now before the Nationalist Party is defeated.'

The clock on the mantelpiece strikes the hour. Robert checks his watch, drains the mug, and stands up, preparing to leave. He turns to brush his lips against Elizabeth's cheek. She straightens the knot of his tie, delaying his departure. She swallows nervously before she speaks.

'It's time for her to come here, Rob. Emmy needs to be with her parents.' Her voice is hushed, pleading. 'She must be growing so fast. It shows in the few photos they send us.' She lifts the locket that, on its silver chain, nestles in the hollow of her throat and holds it up to him. 'See Rob, she has your smile. Let's send for her now.' Unshed tears glisten in her eyes.

He lifts her chin and gazes into her eyes. His expression is grave.

'We have both read the report from the child psychologist. Emmy is loved and being cared for. She's a bright and well-adjusted child. Tearing her away from all she's familiar with will prove too traumatic. Besides, we are still being watched by the authorities.' He rests his cheek on her head. 'Be patient a while longer, my love. Soon we will be reunited.' His voice is thick with emotion.

The scent of his aftershave lingers in her hair long after he has left the room.

Alone, she wanders listlessly around the apartment, clearing the dishes from the breakfast table. The framed photo of their wedding day is prominently displayed on the mantelpiece. She lifts it, holding it up to the morning light. Their happiness is caught in the eye of the camera. She settles into an armchair. Her eyes mist as memories, like gossamer threads, tangle around her and she is catapulted back to the day she and Robert arrived in London.

CHAPTER 22

They disembarked on a cold and drizzly day. The flight from Botswana via Egypt had been long and tedious. In London, a dull, grey sky drained all the colour from the world. It made Elizabeth yearn for the vibrancy of the landscape back home.

On the cab ride from the airport, she sat on the edge of her seat gazing in awe at the city spectacle. She was enraptured by its pulsing energy, its continuous movement, and the grumbling traffic. Robert glanced sideways at her. A slow smile curved his lips. Her childlike response to a city she could never have imagined while living at Tweefontein endeared her to him, and he slipped an arm protectively around her shoulder.

Robert's apartment in the heart of the city was spacious and within walking distance of his office.

David and Anna Moses welcomed Elizabeth and helped pave her way for life in the city. They introduced her to other families in exile and within weeks she was accustomed to the humming city; to streets clogged with people. In time she slipped into the routine of everyday life.

Walking alone through the cool, green parks, she would stop and watch children playing with boats on ponds and the shell of her fragile world cracked as thoughts of Emmy crept in. Who was telling her bedtime stories or kissing a grazed knee? What was her favourite food? Did she wonder about her parents? The unanswered questions twisted her heart with pain. In moments of clarity, she knew that leaving their baby daughter in the care of her parents was the best she and Robert could do for their child, but still grief and guilt consumed her, tears spilling down her cheeks.

Summer was approaching, and the days were warming. Grey skies cleared and were replaced by a tender blue. Elizabeth explored the city. At first, she walked the streets with caution until her forays into London became more confident.

Piccadilly Circus was ablaze with colour. Barrels placed under brightly striped umbrellas were filled with an assortment of flowers, their delicate perfume permeating the air.

"ullo luv,' said the plump-cheeked flower seller with a red kerchief tied beneath her chin. Elizabeth selected a bunch of red, orange and yellow poppies. "ere's one for the 'ubby.' She smiled a gummy smile and handed Elizabeth a long-stemmed red rose. They chatted amicably while Elizabeth searched in her purse for the required money, each entranced by the other's dialect. 'Where ye from luv?' the flower seller enquired. She screwed up her eyes, a bemused expression on her face.

'South Africa,' Elizabeth called over her shoulder as she turned to leave, grinning broadly.

Clutching her bunch of poppies, Elizabeth strolled towards the station enjoying the afternoon sun. A bright-yellow door wedged between two grey high-rise buildings caught her attention. The sign above the door read 'Reader's Nook', a smaller one fixed to a nail read 'Help Wanted'. Gingerly, she pushed against the door. The sound of jangling bells caused her to take a step backward. A face appeared in the crack of the doorway. Blue eyes nestling in a bed of wrinkles radiated kindness. Wispy grey strands had escaped from an untidy bun caught at the nape of her neck and framed the puffy face. A raised eyebrow registered Elizabeth's presence.

'I-I have come about the vacant position,' stuttered Elizabeth.

'Ah then, come in m'love. I was about to take my tea. Join me. Just made egg sandwiches too.'

The open door revealed a short, plump middle-aged woman, her green hand-knitted cardigan stretched across her ample bosom. She was surrounded by shelves stacked with books from floor to ceiling. The musty smell of well-thumbed books clung to the air.

Her name was Nancy Hartley – 'Just call me Nance,' she said. 'Everyone does.' Over freshly brewed tea and egg sandwiches, Elizabeth learned that Mister Hartley had died recently, leaving the second-hand bookstore to his wife. 'But my arthritis has worsened,' she moaned. She spent most of her days in bed in the flatlet behind the store, but still, she was loathe to close the shop. 'My customers are my family.' She looked mournful.

Nancy enjoyed Elizabeth's company, pleased to have an attentive ear to pour out her troubles to. All through tea, Monty, the oversized ginger cat, lay purring in his sleep on Nance's lap. With a sudden fluid motion, he leapt off and nuzzled against Elizabeth's legs

'Oh my,' said Nance, incredulously. 'He likes you. Well, if Monty and I both like you, the job's yours. Can you start tomorrow morning m'luv? I don't pay much, but there are lots of wonderful books to read here.' She winked at Elizabeth.

And, at that moment, an enduring friendship began between the young farm girl from the Cape and the kindly woman from the East End of London.

Commuters thronged the platform of Piccadilly Circus's underground station. The air was filled with the pulsating energy of travellers eager to make their way home. Elizabeth paced the platform impatiently. The wait for the train felt interminable. The poppies she'd purchased from the flower seller were beginning to wilt in the late afternoon warmth. Thoughts of sharing the day's events with Robert created a restless chattering in her head.

Arriving at the apartment, she hastily inserted the key, jiggling it until she registered that the door was unlocked. The patter of water from the shower alerted her to Robert's presence.

'I'm home Rob,' she called, placing the poppies in a jug of water. Then she followed the sound of running water to the bathroom. Robert emerged from the shower, a towel wrapped around his waist, another draped over his wet head. Water glistened on his bare shoulders. He towelled his hair, drops of water splattering against her. She was about to speak when she sensed excitement radiating from him and so she pressed her lips together.

Robert spoke animatedly. 'We've been invited to Paul and Kiara Weiss for Sabbath dinner tomorrow. They suggest we arrive at sundown before candle lighting.'

Nodding eagerly, Elizabeth tapped his chest lightly to gain his attention. 'And I have something to tell you,' she said, with an enigmatic smile.

Robert listened attentively, absorbing her description of Nancy Hartley and her joy at having obtained employment at 'Readers Nook'. He held her gaze for a long moment, a smile playing at the corner of his lips, and laughed heartily at her evocative imitation of Nance.

'Let's celebrate. I'll book a table for dinner tonight at the best restaurant in town.'

CHAPTER 23

Paul Weiss, a merchant banker, had an office in London's central banking district. Despite working for a prestigious company, he was modest and unassuming, with a pleasing face and a ready laugh. Soft brown eyes peered out behind thick-lensed, horn-rimmed glasses. Paul and Robert had met in junior school and were inseparable until Robert was sent to Cape Town to live with relatives after he'd recovered from the accident that killed his father. Their friendship was rekindled when Robert returned to London after having attained a law degree from the University of Cape Town.

Kiara, Paul's wife, was a striking woman of Indian descent and a medical researcher at St George's Hospital. They had met at a political rally when both were studying at university, and they married once their respective families overcame their prejudices – Paul's family being devoutly Jewish while Kiara's were committed Hindus.

Although the weather was cool and a sharp breeze had picked up, Robert and Elizabeth chose to walk the short distance to the Weiss's home.

The route was jammed with revellers celebrating the end of the working week. Pubs overflowed. Patrons spilled out onto the pavement with drinks in hand. Their raucous laughter and rousing greetings mingled with the rumbling traffic.

'You are just in time for the candle lighting,' Kiara said, greeting them warmly at the open door. An oblong metal plaque with Hebrew letters was attached to the righthand door frame. Kiara's long dark hair was rolled into a chignon, accentuating her chiselled cheekbones and aquiline features. Bathed in soft light, her tawny skin appeared luminous.

After the tumult out on the street, the house was an oasis of calm. Kiara steered Elizabeth towards a table on which stood two elaborate silver candlesticks, a lighted candle placed in each one. The candlelight spilled into the room, creating an aura of peace. Elizabeth gazed reverently as Kiara's hands hovered over the flickering flames, her lips moving silently in prayer.

Elizabeth and Robert felt wrapped in the warmth of their hosts.

They gathered around the table which was covered with a pristine white tablecloth. A braided bread placed in the centre was covered with a smaller white cloth. Paul filled a wine goblet with ruby-red wine and intoned the Sabbath blessing, '*Baruch ata adonai eloheinu*'. The stirring words of the ancient ritual echoed through the room, and the wine goblet was passed to each person at the table. The solemn atmosphere was broken when steaming bowls of soup and *perogen* were set on the table giving rise to exclamations of admiration. Succulent grilled salmon on a bed of spinach was served with baby potatoes, and the meal was rounded off with a cinnamon *lokshen* pudding.

The women were alone in the kitchen clearing away the dinner dishes. The men had remained seated at the table, absorbed in discussions related to their respective professions and to the politics of the day.

'There's a rally next week,' Kiara spoke in hushed tones leaning towards Elizabeth. 'Join me in the march. A new campaign is being initiated for Mandela's release and he'll be receiving honours from the British Government. We are meeting at Wembley Stadium.'

Elizabeth turned to Kiara, tears welling up in her eyes. 'The evil of apartheid has torn my family apart and taken my baby from my arms. I'll march until those laws are repealed and democracy is established so that I can return to my family and my country.'

Kiara slipped a consoling arm around her shoulders. An immutable friendship was emerging between the two women, bound by injustice and prejudice.

Much later, when the candles had burned low, Paul escorted them to the door.

Kiara hugged her friend. 'Soon we'll be celebrating Diwali, the festival of light and sweets. It is a ceremony to celebrate the victory of good over evil and is held on a no-moon night, but there will be lots of fireworks. Do join Paul and me.'

It had been an eventful evening and, as it turned out, a pivotal one for Elizabeth.

A fine haze covered the city when Robert and Elizabeth walked the short distance to their apartment. A lamppost along the way was shrouded in mist, creating a halo of golden threads. Robert drew Elizabeth beneath the light and turned her to face him squarely.

'I've made a reservation at the registry office next week. Do you think that your new boss Nancy will allow you time away from the store to get married?' He moistened his lips, apprehensively.

'Robert Booth, are you proposing to me?' Elizabeth's eyes shone.

'Elizabeth Apollos, will you marry me and agree to spend the rest of our lives together?'

Then, like her mother Miemie had before her, Elizabeth raised a beaming face to the moonless sky. With her heart pounding she shouted aloud, 'Yes Robert, I will.'

A rising sun blushed the sky to a delicate pink before it turned gold and spread across the world. Her wedding day was going to be perfect.

It surprised Elizabeth that, regardless of the excitement of the wedding and the accompanying preparations, calmness had settled over her. She had dressed with care and was ready to leave for the registry office. She glanced sideways at Robert and smiled discreetly behind her hand. He was examining his reflection, nervously adjusting the knot in his tie and repeatedly running a comb through his hair.

She walked over to where he stood in front of the full-length mirror. While shaving, he had nicked the skin on his chin and she touched the spot. Abashed, his lopsided smile was enough to fill her heart with love. Elizabeth took a white rose from a vase. The flower seller, whom Elizabeth had befriended, presented it to her for her wedding day. She shortened the stem and slipped it into the lapel of his jacket.

'Now we are ready to be married.'

Hooting from downstairs announced it was time to leave. The taxi driver manoeuvred the car, weaving it through heavy morning traffic. Arriving at the registry office, he opened the door for the bridal couple with a flourish and executed a mock bow before they walked away.

The office was austere. Portraits of past officials, with ceremonial chains adorning their chests, were attached to wood-panelled walls. Dust particles turned to gold in the sunlight that filtered through high window panes.

The registrar sat behind a large, ornate rosewood desk with brass fittings. He wore rimless glasses and had a thinly clipped moustache. Standing, he extended a hand to Robert and Elizabeth in turn and then shuffled the papers on his desk until he was satisfied that he had the relevant forms.

Sensing the gravity of the moment, Elizabeth felt her composure waver. She gripped Robert's hand and took a deep breath to calm her hammering heart.

'Are you ready?' the registrar enquired, peering over the top of his glasses.

'We're waiting for the witnesses to arrive,' answered Robert, looking back nervously at the door through which he and Elizabeth had just entered. Within minutes it flew open, admitting a chorus of raised voices.

'Mazeltov,' called Paul, punching Robert on the shoulder. Behind him stood David and Anna.

The registrar grinned, displaying even white dentures. He smoothed his moustache with thumb and forefinger and adjusted his spectacles. 'Now, are we ready?' He emphasised 'now' in a low, gravelly voice.

Elizabeth stepped forward. There was a collective gasp of admiration as all eyes swept over the radiant bride. Kiara had accompanied Elizabeth to the John Lewis store and they had picked out a buttercup-yellow skirt and matching jacket that highlighted her doe-shaped green eyes and the dark wavy hair that brushed her shoulders. Anna had designed and stitched a matching headpiece with a short veil. A posy of white daisies with streaming white and yellow ribbons was placed in her palms.

The registrar intoned the wedding vows. The 'I dos' were exchanged. Robert slipped a plain gold band onto Elizabeth's fourth finger and the ceremony was complete.

A commotion was heard at the door and again it flew open. The breathless figure of Nancy appeared in the doorway. Her chest heaved with the exertion of climbing the stairs. She embraced Elizabeth.

'I hoped to be here in time for the ceremony,' she spluttered, 'but the morning traffic was heavy.' She removed her purple hat and wiped an arm across her sweating brow. Robert drew up a chair and she dropped into it patting her chest with both hands.

Elizabeth was delighted by Nancy's appearance. 'Who's minding the store?' Her brows drew together.

'No problem,' Nancy said, with a dismissive wave of her hand. 'I attached a sign to the door reading: Getting Married. Back Soon.' Then she laughed at her own joke. The wedding party, unable to suppress their giggles, joined in her infectious merriment. With laughter ringing out, Robert and Elizabeth brushed silver confetti from their shoulders.

The jubilant party, delighted to have witnessed the union of this young and loving couple, made its way to the Ritz Hotel's champagne lounge to continue the celebration.

No one among the guests doubted that the many challenges lying ahead were yet to be overcome.

Alone in their bedroom later that night, Robert gazed at Elizabeth bathed in soft lamplight, her plain white nightgown contrasting with her cinnamon skin. He swept her hair back from her forehead and cupped her face in his palms.

'I managed to send a message to Barney telling him that Emmy's parents are married.'

Then he folded her in his arms.

CHAPTER 24

The strident ring of the telephone stirs her from her reverie. She places the wedding photo she is holding back on the mantelpiece and rubs her eyes to clear the images that dance behind her lids, then she reaches for the receiver.

'There's another strike on the underground,' warns Robert. 'I'll be home late this evening.'

The first raindrops splatter, then trickle down the windowpane. Her eyes search for the umbrella in the hallstand. She decides to wear her blue rain boots.

Before leaving the apartment, she turns back to ensure that the door is securely locked, then opens her bright-red umbrella. The walk to the bus stop is short, but by now the rain is torrential. She steps cautiously over the puddles of rainwater, bracing herself against the icy weather. The bus to Piccadilly Circus grinds slowly through the morning traffic. She will be late for work.

Elizabeth stamps the sleet off her blue boots, closes the red umbrella, and opens the yellow door.

'Morning Nancy,' she sings out. 'I am sorry I'm late. The underground is on strike again.' She bends to stroke Monty. The ginger cat had padded across the room and rubbed his furry body against her legs.

'There you are,' Nancy wheezes, sighing with relief. 'Monty is as happy to see you as I am. It's the old 'rithtist again,' she moans, her face pinched with pain. She holds her hands in front of her and splays out her fingers. The joints are knotted with arthritis. 'Please watch the store today m'luv, I'm feeling poorly. There's hot chocolate on the stove. I'll be at the back should you need me.'

Nancy shuffles her large frame through the door leading to her living quarters behind the store, her slippers making flapping sounds on the wooden floorboards.

Elizabeth fills a mug with hot chocolate. She wraps her hands around its warmth, blowing stream off the top, and settles behind the sturdy table in the middle of the shop. It is stacked with books and serves as a desk and a reading corner. Monty jumps onto her lap, purring loudly.

The bells noisily announce the arrival of the first customer of the day. A rush of frosty air follows the stooped figure through the open doorway. He balances his walking stick against the edge of the table and rubs his gloved hands together.

'Mornin' to you,' he calls.

Elizabeth dislodges Monty and rises to greet him. 'Morning Mister Phillips. Are you coming in to browse? I have a mug of hot chocolate for you.'

'Ah, you are a good girl, Elizabeth,' he sighs, contentedly accepting the mug. He smacks his lips loudly with each sip of the hot drink. 'Any new books? Need one for the missus. With Christmas just around the corner . . .' his voice drones on.

Christmas. The word hangs in the air. Emmy's fifth birthday. Elizabeth's heart flutters like the wings of a captured bird.

Mr Phillips's voice drifts around her while he randomly pages through the books on the table, but only one word has registered: Christmas.

Having drained his mug, the old man collects his walking stick and prepares to leave.

'You all right child?' he asks, peering shortsightedly at her and, noticing her fixed expression, pats her arm. 'I'll be back tomorrow. Tell Nancy I say hello.'

The bells sound once more as the door slams shut behind him.

Daylight is waning when Elizabeth closes the yellow door and leaves for home. Moisture in the air clings to her clothing and shines like little stars in the fading light. She turns her collar up against the damp and sets out for the bus stop.

The shop windows are dressed in dazzling Christmas displays. Sleds filled with toys and driven by bearded Santas are airborne in the windows; silver tinsel surrounds fireplaces in which flames dance, and tables are laid in readiness for a feast. The joy of Christmas is alluring. Her thoughts ricochet to Tweefontein and the different Christmas those on the farm will experience in the stifling heat of the valley.

In her mind, she talks to Emmy, selecting a doll from the vast selection on display in the window. She tries to imagine a five-year-old Emmy. *Has she lost a baby tooth yet?*

Five years have passed and still she lives with the pain, like an aching limb.

The following afternoon, Elizabeth, Anna and Kiara take part in a planned march. Pressure on South Africa is intensifying. The threat of international boycotts looms. Elizabeth's convictions harden. Her dream of returning to South Africa is beginning to feel tangible.

They march in groups through the streets of London, forming a phalanx of pulsating energy. It takes them past houses, many with their window panes set behind hedges. In others, they view domestic scenes and then they march into the frenetic movement of the high streets. They hold their banners up, protesting vehemently. 'Free Mandela!' is the message being delivered through loudhailers and echoed by speakers standing on boxes in the leafy green parks of London. Among the throng of marchers is a palpable determination to bring about democracy in a non-racial South Africa.

Away from the churn of the crowd, in the mellow light of day's end, she returns to the apartment. Although pale with fatigue she is bright-eyed. The image of Emmy cradled in her arms is crystallising in her imagination. She greets Robert smiling contentedly.

CHAPTER 25

During the night a fine drift of snow had blanketed the landscape, frosting the tops of trees and bushes. Ribbons of predawn light cast a ghostly glow. The silence felt timeless.

It was Christmas morning.

Elizabeth woke to the sound of rattling pots coming from the kitchen. Robert was preparing lunch. A large stuffed turkey, potatoes and mince pies were simmering in the oven, the mouth-watering smells wafted temptingly through the apartment. 'Another Christmas,' she yawned, and stretched luxuriously. It was the measure of her years away from home.

The days before Christmas had seen a flurry of customers in Reader's Nook, keeping Elizabeth on her feet and the tills ringing. Nancy was delighted with her ability to lure customers inside and to conclude sales.

She padded barefoot into the kitchen and stood behind Robert, circling her arms around his waist. She laid her cheek against his back. 'Merry Christmas, my love,' she said, her voice throaty with sleep. He turned to face her, gently reaching for her chin and lifting her face towards his.

'Today I am the chef.' He chuckled. 'Please would you set out the lunch table before our guests arrive?'

Elizabeth glanced at the wall clock, her eyes widening, 'I'll have to hurry, they'll be here soon.' She transformed the apartment, creating a festive air. Silver cutlery gleamed on a white tablecloth and tiny coloured lights flickered on a miniature tree in the corner of the room.

The smack of wet rain boots announced the arrival of Paul, Kiara, and Nancy.

'Tis me mum's recipe,' said Nancy handing Elizabeth a covered dish. 'Made the pudding m'self. It's full of cranberries and nuts and lots of Port.' She winked, before settling into a comfortable seat, shuffling her feet apart. She adjusted a brightly patterned shawl across her shoulders. Paul passed glasses of deep-red wine around and then he placed another bottle in the centre of the table. Framed photos of Emmy were admired and opinions aired on which parent she most resembled. The turkey was carved, crackers burst and gifts were exchanged. But, as the bottles of wine emptied, it was their friendship that warmed the room.

Soon it would be New Year's Eve.

A sleek black vehicle was parked in the street beneath the apartment. Robert had recently joined a carpool and had the use of the car until the following day, New Year's Day. Instead of hailing a taxi, he and Elizabeth drove themselves comfortably to attend David and Anna's party that evening.

Sleet covered the roads and pathways, the frosty air trembled in the gusting wind.

They were greeted by the Moses children who flung their arms around Robert's legs, eager to be lifted and swung around, the littlest hoisted up onto his shoulders. It was a familiar game enacted whenever they visited.

Guests were gathered around a roaring fire. A tall Christmas tree, ablaze with fairy lights, dominated the room. Women in shiny evening dresses swished around it, admiring the decorations and the angel placed precariously on top. The men hunkered around the fireplace. Tales abounded of past Christmases celebrated at home. The women, lured by the warmth of the fire and the stories being animatedly exchanged, drifted towards the group of men. Their appetite for news from South Africa was insatiable and their memories intact. Although most of the exiles had been living in London for many years, they still considered their stay to be temporary. They believed fervently that the Nationalist Government would soon collapse and be replaced by a just administration, allowing them to return to their homeland.

Wine flowed as the evening progressed. The conversation became robust as the alcohol unmasked hidden emotions, and memories became more vivid. And yet, a chasm separated those memories from the moment that they now celebrated, far from relatives and friends.

The women moved into the kitchen to prepare the evening meal. The conversation among the men seated around the fire became more urgent. Political matters were hotly discussed. Resistance in South Africa was deepening, activists were becoming bolder. David drew up his seat, beckoning with his head to the men to come closer. He leaned forward, placing his hands on his knees, and dropped his voice. There was a hard edge to his features.

'I have received an intelligence report,' he began, his dark eyes warily scanning the group. 'Spies from South Africa's secret police have infiltrated refugees and exiles living in London. Their true identities are unknown but they are very convincing. The situation is dangerous.' The men listened in rapt attention. Although they were stony-faced, the glow from the fire reflected the fear in their eyes. There was a spine-chilling sense of a lurking malevolence.

The sombre mood lifted when the men were called to the dinner table. The rich aroma of roast meats and buttered potatoes filled the room. Eagerly they gathered around the table, their friendship cemented by the challenges that had brought them together.

'Look,' the children's voices rang out, pointing at a bay window. An explosion of red, gold and silver stars lit up the inky sky. In the spectacle of the firework display from Putney Bridge, all thoughts of danger were temporarily put aside. 'Happy New Year!' they cried out in unison. They embraced, but each heart harboured a secret prayer.

It was 1984.

Arriving at his office in the morning after David and Anna's New Year's Eve party, Robert found a faxed message placed on his desk. The threat was stark: You are named on the secret police's hit list. Be warned.

It was unsigned.

CHAPTER 26

TWEEFONTEIN

The weathered brick house on the hill close to the stream is transformed with the arrival of baby Emmy. Nappies flap on the clothesline and the walls inside echo with the baby's gurgles.

Karel and Miemie are enthralled with their granddaughter who is a contented and placid child. She grows rapidly and each milestone is celebrated. A new tooth or first word is cause for celebration on Tweefontein. Soon Miemie hefts the baby up on her thrust hip and walks to the homestead. Emmy circles an arm around her grandmother's neck, reaches for an earlobe, and rests her head on the familiar shoulder, her thumb in her mouth. The farmhouse kitchen is warm and filled with the aroma of the contents of pots bubbling on the stove. Miemie, keeping a watchful eye on the child sleeping in a basinette at her feet, peels, cuts and chops the vegetables from the farm garden. The farmhouse kitchen is redolent with smells that trigger memories of Elizabeth.

Her departure has left her parents with an aching sense of loss. Lack of communication increases their fear. Barney has assumed the role of a devoted uncle and visits the Apollos home frequently, plying the child with gifts. His assurances that Elizabeth and Robert are well, and are safe in London, helps to ease their anxiety.

Emmy fills the void left by Elizabeth. Karel is absorbed with the child. He bounces her, swinging her up in the air. She kicks her little legs, chuckling and demanding more until they are both breathless with laughter.

A weight begins to shift off Karel and Miemie as Emmy emerges from babyhood to childhood.

Still a carefree toddler she is, as yet, untouched by the future.

Freda and Dirk have slipped contentedly into the sunset of their lives. Tweefontein has thrived, the harvest yield increases yearly, and their wines win accolades at home and abroad, the most successful being their Chardonnay. The word 'Chardonnay', derived from the Hebrew Sha'ar Adonai, means Gate of God.

Dirk Junior – Dirkie – lives with his wife Janet and their two daughters in Johannesburg where he runs a successful law practice. Helene has recently graduated with honours as a psychologist from Stellenbosch University. Their children's accomplishments have added to their sense of abundance.

It is the Easter vacation and the homestead, where the family is gathered, is a hive of activity. In the kitchen, Miemie and Katie are conjuring up chocolate desserts and sweet treats. The tempting fragrance drifts throughout the house.

Autumn has transformed the green of summer into shades of yellow and gold. A gentle breeze blows the flowers from their stems, scattering the petals. The Coetzee men each drive small tractors through the vineyards to inspect the late grape harvest. Freda and Helene lounge in comfortable silence beneath the oak trees. A narrow shaft of light filters through the branches. The dry leaves rustle and the sharp smell of freshly cut grass slices through the air.

The aura of peace is shattered by the shouts of children as they chase each other around the trees in search of Easter eggs. A smile of satisfaction crosses Freda's face as she watches them play. Emmy is among them. She turns to Helene.

'Emmy has grown into a bonny child. She has brought joy to Karel and Miemie as well as to all of us on the farm.'

'Where are her parents?' Helene wrinkles her brow into a deep frown.

Freda raises her shoulders, her palms turned up. 'There's been no word from either of them, but we know that they're on the hit list of the secret police. Your father receives information that makes us fear for their safety.'

Helene remains contemplative. When she speaks, it is in a measured tone. 'Emmy is young and oblivious of the situation she has been born into. Being raised by Karel and Miemie in a childhood that includes you, Pa, Zelda and Barney will present challenges.' She folds her arms across her chest and stares through narrowed eyes into the distance, as though searching for answers. The minutes tick by before she speaks again. When she does, her voice is filled with compassion. 'I predict that Emmy will always carry something unresolved within her.' She turns to face Freda. 'Are you aware that the farmworkers refer to her as Witkind?'

'I want to . . . I want to . . .' six-year-old Emmy wails, beating her little fists against Oumie's chest. Her face is puckered and wet with tears of frustration. 'I want to go to school with Boetie and Amelia' – Ousis's grandchildren – 'I don't want to go to the school for white children,' she sobs. Miemie gathers the child up enclosing her flailing arms with her own, holding Emmy against her bosom. Sorrow clouds her eyes. Karel is right, she thinks. Emmy is confused. We need to tell her before it is too late.

Emmy, emotionally spent and exhausted, lies whimpering in her Oumie's arms. Miemie settles into the same chair in which she nursed Emmy as an infant and soothingly hums a few bars of a Brahms lullaby. She searches for the right words.

'You are fortunate to attend Malansdorp Primary School. You will learn so much that you will be able to teach Pa and me.'

Emmy smiles through her tears. 'Where did you go to school, Oumie?' she says, nestling against Miemie, her thumb firmly planted in her mouth.

'I went to the school for coloured kids. I didn't learn as much as you will. I left school when I was fourteen to work in the farmstall. The money I earned helped Ma.'

'Will you take me to the school for white kids in the morning, Oumie?'

'No, my *liefie*. Tannie Freda will take you. She will tell Miss Simms, your teacher, that you are her niece.'

Emmy's face crumples, more tears threatening.

'But, child, when school comes out at the end of the day, you will come home to Pa and me. This is where you belong,' Miemie says defiantly.

The country town, Malansdorp, bristled with activity. It was the much-anticipated Annual Church Bazaar.

Outside the church hall, children mounted on ponies were shrieking with delight. Inside, their elders hefted baskets with the weight of recently purchased confectionery and cakes.

In an area reserved for barbecuing boerewors rolls, well-muscled men pitted their strength against each other in a high-stake contest of egos.

'Legs Eleven!' called the bingo master, followed by a triumphant 'yes' from the attentive players.

In a far corner, Dalene de Wet and Gerda Rust sat at a table covered with a lace cloth. They nibbled at the doughnuts and vetkoek heaped in the centre of the table, occasionally sipping coffee from dainty rose-patterned cups.

Dalene shifted her bulky frame to get a better view of the cake stall. She sighed in satisfaction. The chiffon and chocolate cakes she'd baked in her kitchen were rapidly disappearing, the first to be sold.

'Another successful bazaar,' she smiled smugly, turning to face Gerda who nodded her agreement.

Gerda was about to lift another chocolate doughnut to her heavily rouged lips when she caught sight of Freda Coetzee in conversation with the Pastor. She dropped the doughnut and nudged Dalene. 'Look who's there?' Her eyes lit up with the anticipation of gossip.

'There's a new child in my Hanalie's class. Her name is Emmy Booth,' said Dalene.

Gerda placed her hand at the side of her mouth, speaking out the corner of it. 'She's supposed to be Freda and Dirk Coetzee's niece but there are rumours' – she lowered her voice – 'that she has a touch of the tar brush.' She pressed her lips together, flattening her chins.

Dalene's gaze lingered on Freda. 'I've also heard the rumours. Something to do with the farmworkers. The young coloured people these days are getting out of control, says my Willie.' Her voice trailed off as she continued to scrutinise Freda. 'Emmy is a nice enough child,' she continued. 'My Hanalie was invited for a play date at the Coetzee's farmhouse.'

Gerda frowned. 'I'm sure my Sissie will be invited too.' She shrugged her shoulders while flouncing out the stiff curls of her latest hairdo. 'My Danie and Dirk Coetzee are both members of the Broederbond. Dirk would never break the law,' she added, emphatically.

Dalene was thoughtful, slowly chewing the last bit of vetkoek. She dabbed the paper serviette delicately at the corners of her mouth, 'My Willie thinks Dirk Coetzee has left-leaning tendencies.'

Freda walked up to the table, interrupting their conversation.

'Hello ladies,' she greeted the women.

'Oh helloo-o Freda,' they chorused in unison, jumping up to greet her.

'How's your little niece?' enquired Dalene, solicitously.

'Do send her to play with my Sissie,' simpered Gerda.

Freda nodded and, with a complacent smile, turned away.

CHAPTER 27

Emmy anticipated her seventh birthday with a mixture of joy and profound sadness. She counted the days to when Zelda's Datsun would arrive at Tweefontein and she would leave with her to spend the day in the city. Knowing that Oumie and Pa would not join them made her sad.

Oumie had washed and ironed Emmy's Sunday dress in preparation for the visit. On the morning of her birthday, she carefully parted and braided Emmy's abundant blonde hair into pigtails, securing them with blue bows, the same forget-me-not blue of Emmy's eyes.

The sun had barely risen when the Datsun drew up to the house, trailing a plume of dust along the dirt road. Zelda stepped out, 'Hello-o' she sang out, smiling happily and throwing her hands up in greeting. She hugged Karel and Miemie. 'Now come along Emmy,' she said guiding her into the back seat of the car. Snapping the safety belt around her, she revved the engine ready to leave. Sitting on the back seat, clutching her pink Barbie backpack, Emmy twisted back to wave at Oumie and Pa. She had seen the sorrow in their eyes when she had left, holding Zelda's hand. She felt she was abandoning them.

'I wish Oumie and Pa could come with us,' she whimpered, her bottom lip trembling.

Zelda glanced in the rear-view mirror and spoke consolingly. 'The law allows only white people like you and me to enter the restaurant and cinema that we will be going to. It is sad Emmy. I hope that the law will soon change. But,' she added, brightening, 'Barney will be joining us for lunch.'

Emmy mulled over the information Zelda had provided. She was coming to terms with the strange world into which she had, by an accident of birth, been thrust. The people she most loved were unable to gather together because of the colour of their skin, a law she was not able to comprehend. She felt her eyes begin to tear but she steeled herself. Her best friend, Marie, had called her a crybaby because she sobbed when Tannie Freda accompanied her to school in the morning instead of Oumie. Now she was seven years old and nearly grown up. She brushed away her tears. Emmy was learning measured ways to suppress her tears and conceal her emotions.

The sun was steadily rising when Zelda's car drew up to Devil's Peak and arrived at the house on Magnolia Street. Zelda surprised Emmy with her own freshly decorated bedroom. She had chosen a bed with a frilly pink canopy and matching pink blinds. Scatter rugs were placed on the wooden floor and the shelves were lined with books. It felt welcoming and intimate. Overjoyed, Emmy lifted a book off the shelf and pulled Zelda onto the bed beside her. Time passed as Zelda read to her from *A Child's Garden of Verse*. Emmy loved the sound of Zelda's gravelly voice. The staccato rhythm of Hilaire Beloc's poem 'Tarantella' drifted her into a world of fantasy.

The day had only begun, the morning was still magical, when Zelda winged her elbow, and Emmy threaded her arm through and they ambled down the avenue running through the city's Company Gardens. The exotic purple and red blooms on leafy boughs formed an overhead cover for picnickers who lounged on the lush green lawns. Tame squirrels with bushy tails nibbled on peanuts that were scattered along the pathway. It made Emmy giggle when they nibbled the nuts from her cupped palm.

Synchronised voices of a choir celebrating the Sabbath in a morning service floated towards them from the nearby synagogue. They rested on a wooden bench, adrift in the celestial sounds. The pavements of Adderley Street became clogged with late-morning shoppers. People waited patiently in queues to board red double-decker buses. Shop windows displayed the latest fashion and billboards the day's news. Christmas decorations lit up the length of the thoroughfare.

A stark black-and-white billboard positioned above a news stand read: Four stone-throwing youths killed by police in Athlone.

Emmy saw the pain reflected in Zelda's face when she paused in front of it. She slipped her hand into Zelda's to console her while quietly scuffing the toe of her shoe. Zelda purchased the newspaper from the vendor and tucked it beneath her arm, but her eyes remained clouded.

They were seated in the corner of the crowded restaurant when Barney arrived. He stood at the entrance, his eyes raking the room until he spotted the two and hurried towards the table. His face was florid from the heat, the buttons of his short-sleeved shirt straining against his expanding girth. Auburn tufts grew around an otherwise bald and shiny head. He radiated excitement.

'Happy birthday, my love,' he chuckled, lifting Emmy off the seat and spinning her around. He placed a small white box in her hand. Intrigued, she tugged at the pink ribbon around it and it opened. Inside, a silver locket lay on purple velvet folds. Emmy's eyes lit up. This locket was to become a cherished possession throughout her life. She did not know then that in the hollow of her mother's throat lay a similar one in which a picture of her was framed.

Barney, seated at the table, turned to Zelda. He clenched his jaw and dropped his voice. 'My home was raided last night.'

Zelda gasped in horror. 'Did they find anything incriminating?'

He patted her arm reassuringly. 'I had a warning and was able to destroy those files before they arrived. They found nothing of importance, mainly lists of my medical reports,' he grinned. 'But be warned,' he added, 'we must have no contact with London. The security police are unsettled and dangerous. Thousands have been detained.'

Zelda tapped the newspaper that she'd placed on the table, drawing his attention to the headlines, and nodded in agreement.

Before it was time to leave, Barney beckoned to the waiter who placed a dish of ice cream lit up with sparklers on the table before Emmy. 'Make a wish,' Barney instructed her.

Emmy's eyes were squeezed shut in concentration, her lashes brushing her cheeks. Then, beaming, she looked up, 'I wish that next year Oumie and Pa can join us,' she said, unhesitatingly.

CHAPTER 28

This is the coldest winter,' they said. 'It hasn't been this cold for the past ten years, not since 1975,' they said, turning up the collars of their padded jackets and blowing on their hands.

Yellow-grey smoke curled from chimney tops into a colourless sky. Gusts of wind howled off snowcapped mountains into the valley causing the inhabitants to burrow down in their homes behind closed doors. The glow of coals in braziers flickered against windowpanes, streaming light into a leaden world.

In the town, tensions were perceptible. Folk gathered on the town square and street corners. 'Have you heard?' was the common refrain, as they searched each other's faces, their eyes filled with hope.

'It's the end of apartheid,' said some jubilantly, while others shook their heads and lowered their eyes. 'You can't trust President Botha.'

'But,' a chorus of voices declared, 'Nelson Mandela will be released when President Botha delivers his speech tonight.'

In the farmhouse, Freda and Dirk drew their seats up close to the television screen. Glowing logs crackled and sighed in the hearth. Dirk rose and stoked the fire, using a brass poker that hung off a hook on the red brick surround of the hearth. He glanced at his watch, eyeing the television screen nervously.

'Soon,' he nodded at Freda and settled into a wing-backed chair, crossing his hands, his legs stretched out in front of him.

Then President Botha's face flashed onto the screen.

In the Apollos home, tension was etched onto the faces of the occupants. They, too, turned up the sound of the television set, hoping for the message that would alter their lives and bring their daughter home. Miemie lay curled up on the couch. She shivered in anticipation and drew a shawl close across her shoulders. Emmy lay sleeping against her, tucked into the warm curve of her body. Restlessly, Karel switched channels and adjusted the sound as he paced the room.

Then President Botha's face flashed onto the screen.

Thabu joined Zelda and Barney in the sitting room of the house on Magnolia Street. He slipped in quietly through the back door, his beanie pulled low over his brow. His shoulders were hunched into his jacket. He folded his arms across his chest placing his hands in his armpits and stamped his feet against the cold. 'Hello,' he called out to announce his arrival.

Strong coffee bubbled in a percolator. The room was dimly lit, the shades pulled down. Thabu poured coffee into a mug and grabbed a rusk from a plate close by. He settled on the couch between Barney and Zelda, facing the television screen, and let out a long sigh of contentment.

'Bro, what do you think President Botha will say in his speech tonight?' queried Barney turning to Thabu. Thabu remained thoughtful, his fists were clenched. The clock ticked loudly in the silence. His eyes swivelled from Barney to Zelda and he gave a rueful smile before he answered.

'I believe that the president won't change anything. He steadfastly believes in white supremacy and has too much to lose.' He added soberly, 'Our fight will intensify.'

Then President Botha's face flashed onto the screen.

In London, sunset painted the skyline muted shades of gold and crimson. It had been a blisteringly hot day, the heat rising off the pavements. At the Hog and Hare pub, revellers congregated, enjoying the good weather. They spilled out onto the pavement with drinks in hand. In the middle of the jostling crowd, a group gathered in front of the television screen. Unlike the roisters, their expressions were solemn.

Robert glanced up at the wood-framed clock on the wall. The face had yellowed with age. He slipped an arm around Elizabeth. Meeting Paul and David's eyes, he nodded imperceptibly. 'Any moment now,' he mouthed, avoiding the background noise that drowned out his words.

When President Botha's face flashed on the screen, a hush fell across the room and all eyes swivelled to the television set.

Across continents, President Botha's voice droned as communities held their collective breath. Then, with his finger wagging, his voice boomed, 'I am not going to hand South Africa over to these revolutionaries. I believe that we are today crossing the Rubicon. There can be no turning back.'

The world fell silent.

Karel, his face dark with fury, balled one hand into a fist and punched it into the opposite palm. He swore under his breath as he turned down the sound.

In the farmhouse, Dirk glanced at Freda, lifting his shoulders. 'The president must surely be aware of the damage his speech will cause. Be prepared for more unrest. South Africa will be in turmoil.'

Ignoring the drama being displayed on the television screen, Freda studied Dirk. She noted that his hairline had receded and his chin was beginning to sag.

'Have you observed how frail Karel Apollos has become lately?' she said.

'He does seem to be unwell. I've instructed Dirkie to cede the title deeds to their home and the land around it to Miemie and Karel.'

Freda moved across the room to where Dirk sat and threaded her arms around his neck. 'You're a good man, my husband.'

She turned down the lights.

Barney, his face set with a look of resignation, prepared to leave.

'I think I'll sleep on your couch tonight, Zelda. If I may?' asked Thabu.

Zelda's lips were drawn into a thin line, her expression was troubled. 'Help yourself Thabu, the blankets are in the cupboard.'

Then she, too, turned down the lights.

In the Hog and Hare, Elizabeth, Kiara and Anna clasped hands. Tears slid noiselessly down Elizabeth's cheeks. Robert beckoned to the bartender: 'Another round of drinks for the table, please.'

In the situation room in the White House, the president, in slippers and a dressing gown, was slowly stirring his early morning mug of hot chocolate in front of the television screen. He was surrounded by journalists. President Botha, the South African president, had just delivered his much-anticipated speech.

'Any comment, Mister President?' A young blonde woman held out a microphone to him.

The president raised the mug to his lips, gazing thoughtfully over the rim. 'I think that the time has come to intensify sanctions against South Africa.'

The journalists left the room.

CHAPTER 29

LONDON
1992

The first rays of the sun broke through a mesh of purple and grey clouds that swept across the London sky.

Alone in his office, Robert nervously chewed on a thumbnail. He paced, glancing alternatively at his watch and the telephone. The sounds of early morning traffic in the street below drifted up to him. Then a soft cooing sound outside the window drew his attention. A grey dove was perched on the windowsill.

'Hello, my friend,' he said, gently tapping against the pane. The dove cocked its head quizzically and gazed at Robert. It hopped from one foot to the other, then turned around, fluffed out its tail feathers, and flew away.

A bird is a sign of freedom, Robert thought meditatively, watching the bird arc high across the sky.

The scraping sound of a key in the lock of the outer office alerted him and he turned from the window. David entered the office holding a newspaper at arm's length towards Robert. It was a copy of South Africa's *Cape Times*. The headlines – **It's Yes!** – were splashed across the front page in bold black letters.

Robert exhaled. His shoulders slumped with released tension. A pulse throbbed in the base of his throat.

'President de Klerk's referendum is a success. Apartheid will be abolished and a new government voted in. The date of the election will be announced,' said David joyfully.

Claire Mullins entered the office carrying a tray of steaming coffee mugs. A cacophony of ringing telephones and clattering typewriters followed her through the doorway.

It was the beginning of a new day.

The outer door of the office flew open again accompanied by a rush of footsteps. Paul appeared, framed in the doorway, breathlessly brandishing a newspaper. He had run a short distance from his office. 'See this,' he said, triumphantly stabbing a finger at the headlines before folding himself into an office chair. The euphoria felt by the men was palpable.

David wrapped his hands around a mug. He became pensive as he slowly sipped the warm drink. 'The referendum has brought us hope, but the situation in South Africa is still fraught with danger. Our group outside the country has worked tirelessly to bring about this revolution. Funding to opposition parties has provided them with armaments and ammunition. Now right-wing groups will become more prominent as they oppose the president's stance. Gentlemen,' he said, slapping the table for emphasis, 'the war is not over yet. Robert and I are on the most-wanted list held by far-right parties. They are hell-bent on revenge.'

David's sobering words did not dampen Robert's joy. 'I'll be meeting my daughter at last,' he said, snatching up the receiver of the telephone on his desk. He dialled quickly and efficiently. In the apartment, an anxious Elizabeth answered on the first ring.

'What's the outcome of the referendum?' she breathed into the receiver.

'It's Yes! Soon we'll be going home to be reunited with Emmy.' His voice rose with excitement. Although she could not see his face, she knew he was grinning, his grin becoming broader.

Paul and David put their empty mugs back on the tray and with quick handshakes turned to leave.

Alone in his office, Robert's attention was again drawn to birdsong coming from outside the window.

The dove had returned.

CHAPTER 30

1993

Malansdorp School for Girls, was a stately old building dating back to the nineteenth century and dominated the small country town. Generations of young girls had passed from childhood to adulthood through its hallowed portals.

That night the school hall was packed with theatregoers. Billboards advertising the production of the musical *Annie* had been prominently displayed throughout the town. Emmy Booth was in the starring role.

A current of excitement ran through the hall as patrons, their programmes rustling, filed in to take their seats. When the lights dimmed and the curtain rose, an expectant hush fell over the audience. Emmy, in a curly red wig, appeared centre stage illuminated in a pool of floodlight. Her pitch-perfect voice belted out the headline song 'Tomorrow', the notes swirling towards the ceiling. The audience was captivated.

'She's a natural,' whispered Barney, leaning towards Zelda who sat next to him. She smiled, hearing the pride in his voice.

The final curtain fell and the crowd rose to its feet in thunderous applause. The show was a success.

Zelda and Barney, together with the Coetzees, waited in the foyer for Emmy to emerge from backstage. 'Miemie and Karel should be here tonight. They'd be so proud of Emmy,' Zelda said.

Dirk Coetzee looked around uncomfortably at the 'whites only' audience. Miemie and Karel were alone at home, although the laws were slowly being repealed they were still ill at ease.

'She's talented,' Zelda continued. 'We must encourage her to enroll at UCT's drama school when she's finished her schooling this year.'

'She wants to make acting her career,' Freda said. Then she moved closer and threaded her arm companionably through Zelda's. She spoke hesitantly, addressing her fears. 'We have to tell her about her parents. She was too young and vulnerable to have been burdened with dangerous secrets, but now she's older and it's time for her to know the truth about her past. Now that F.W. de Klerk's referendum to end apartheid has succeded. Robert and Elizabeth will be coming home to meet their daughter and Emmy must be prepared for this meeting.'

A heavy silence hung between the women. Zelda gazed into the distance, her jaw set. Then she patted Freda's arm and nodded. 'The decision must be Karel and Miemie's. I'll discuss it with them.'

The silence hangs heavy in the air, made denser by the stillness of the figures seated around the kitchen table. Zelda, nursing a mug of cocoa in her palms, faces Karel and Miemie. Karel, head bowed, fidgets with the tablecloth. Miemie stares stonily ahead. Fear darkens her eyes.

A clock strikes in the distance and Zelda glances at her wristwatch, noting that half an hour has elapsed since she arrived at their cottage to deliver her message to Karel and Miemie Apollos.

She breaks the silence and repeats the message. She is persuasive.

'Now that she's older, it's time for Emmy to know the truth about her past. She has a right to know, Miemie. You and

Karel have to tell her.' She eyes them shrewdly, understanding their anguish.

Then her voice softens. 'Miemie, you have our support.' She has a fleeting impulse to hold Miemie in her arms.

Miemie bites her lower lip, and says, 'We'll lose her.'

'Miemie, you and Karel have been her anchor and security. She may be angry for a while, but Emmy is even-tempered and good-natured, and she loves you both deeply. The bonds that bind you to her can never be broken. Be brave, Miemie, tell Emmy. You owe it to her.'

Miemie turns to Karel and takes his hand in her own. Different emotions fighting for dominance cross her face. When she speaks, her voice is firm. '*Ons sal* – we will tell her. Zelda is right. It's time for her to know about her parents before they return for her.'

Zelda exhales heavily. The sigh comes from deep inside her.

Emmy sits crossed-legged on the couch. Karel and Miemie sit facing her. Photographs and newspaper cuttings are strewn around the couch, some falling onto the ground. Emmy holds up a photograph of Elizabeth. She is mesmerised by the image. This is her mother. The soft glow of lamplight that flickers across her face reveals the confusion in her eyes. The silence of the night pulses around them, broken only by the staccato tapping of raindrops on the roof.

Emmy's gaze shifts from Karel to Miemie. She has lost track of time. Their words are fleeting shadows she cannot hold onto. The story of her childhood feels like a dream that is slowly dissolving. She draws a deep breath. Her throat constricts, stalling the questions on her lips.

'Why didn't you tell me about my mother and father and the reason they abandoned me?' Her voice is thin and high, she's holding back tears. She exhales and her shoulders slump. Anger and frustration leave her limp.

The silence stretches between them. Karel leans forward, his arms resting on his knees, his hands clasped. He searches his armoury to find the right words. 'Oumie and I wanted to protect you from a dangerous situation that you were too young to grasp – because we love you . . .' His voice disappears into nothingness.

Somewhere in the distance, a shutter bangs in the wind, again and again.

Miemie rises and moves across to where Emmy sits on the couch. Gently she turns Emmy to face her unflinching gaze. 'Forgive us, child.'

Her words ring hollow in her ears, but it is all she has to give the girl she dearly loves.

After the secrets of her childhood are revealed, Emmy's demeanour changes perceptibly. Her wide blue eyes shine with clarity and she moves with a confident and assertive stride. A veil has been lifted on suppressed anxieties and unanswered questions. She views her life through a new prism. Yet doubts still linger.

The thud of a satchel dropping onto the floor announces her arrival in the cottage at the end of the school day. She greets Miemie and settles at the kitchen table. Miemie places a dish of meatballs wrapped in cabbage leaves on a bed of lentils on the table.

'Eat, my child,' she instructs Emmy.

Miemie sits facing Emmy, her elbows are on the table, her chin resting in her cupped palms. She swallows nervously before she speaks. 'Emmy, you have the choice of living with Zelda and finishing your schooling in the city. It might provide you with more opportunities than you'll have in Malansdorp. Besides, you'll be able to apply for drama school.' Her words come out in a rush.

Emmy puts down the cutlery she holds. They clatter onto the plate. She folds her hands in her lap and looks directly at Miemie.

'I want to stay with you and Pa. This is my home.'

In that moment, all her uncertainties dissolve and she eats her meal with Miemie beside her, the two drawn together by deep bonds of love.

CHAPTER 31

TWEEFONTEIN

Dirk Coetzee stood in bright sunlight, surveying the vineyards. The vines were set out in perpendicular rows as far as the eye could see. He squinted into the light and adjusted the wide brim of his straw hat. Licking a forefinger, he held it up and turned to face the wind.

'Rain's coming,' he murmured.

Noticing the heavy clusters of late-harvest grapes bulging on the vines, he placed his hands on his hips and smiled with satisfaction. The crunch of tyres on the gravel pathway caused him to turn around. Karel was steering a tractor towards him.

'*Goeie more Meneer*, good morning, sir,' Karel waved his hat at Dirk.

Dirk strode up, offering his hand to assist Karel off the high tractor seat. He was alarmed by how laborious Karel's movements were. Once so agile, he now manoeuvred himself with caution, his mobility had decreased rapidly in recent years.

Dirk selected a vine and plucked a bunch of low-hanging grapes. He bit into a sun-ripened berry, the juice spilling down the sides of his mouth, and then he handed the bunch to Karel. 'What is your assessment of the harvest?'

Karel's eyes narrowed thoughtfully. He rolled the juice around his mouth before answering. 'The red will be a good harvest this year, Meneer. The green will have to ripen a bit longer.'

'We'll have to hurry the picking process. Rain will be coming soon.'

In the distance, a figure waved at them. Miemie, purposeful in her stride, cut across the gravel pathway, her apron flapping in the slight breeze. She carried a wicker basket with both hands.

'Karel, I have brought your lunch,' she panted.

Reaching for it, Karel stumbled and dropped the basket. Rivulets of sweat trickled down his forehead and his hands trembled. Dirk took him by the shoulders to steady him and turned to face Miemie, his face creased with worry.

'It's time for Karel to pay a visit to Doc Joe.'

A cloud crossed Miemie's face, her brows drew together. 'I've been telling him to go see the doctor, but he won't admit he's not well. He's obstinate – *hard koppig*.' She clenched her fists in exasperation. 'But now I will make sure he does.' She turned away and with a determined flounce of her head walked back up the gravel pathway. Karel looked sheepishly at Dirk.

'Wives know best,' Dirk said sagely and held out his hand.

Karel took the offered hand and climbed back onto the tractor. He looked down at Dirk. 'I'll go to the doctor tomorrow.' He sighed in resignation. 'I have not yet won an argument with Miemie.'

Wispy clouds had begun to form on the horizon.

Dirk watched Karel and the tractor disappear around a bend in the road. A sense of foreboding settled on him.

A figure appeared from between the vines. Pietman Latief stood up holding a bushel basket filled with red and green grapes. He settled the basket on the ground and doffed his straw hat, holding it reverently to his breast. '*Meneer*,' he greeted Dirk with his eyes downcast. 'The workers are concerned about Karel's health. He breathes with difficulty and he fainted last week, but he insists he is well.'

'I'm also worried, Pietman. I will make certain that the doctor examines him tomorrow.'

Pietman turned his hat around, before replacing it and lifting the basket.

'*Kyk, Meneer,*' he said, pointing with his chin.

The wicker basket containing Karel's lunch remained on the sandy path where Miemie had placed it.

Doctor Joe Marcus held a glass vial up to the light that streamed in through his surgery window. In his other hand, he held the report he'd received with Karel's medical test results. He turned his head from side to side, his lips pursed. There was a grim set to his features.

Karel and Miemie sat stiffly at the desk. Miemie wrung her hands while Karel nervously plucked at the collar of his shirt. Occasionally, he patted her hand. Both stared straight ahead.

Turning from the window, Doc Joe sat down at his desk facing them. He looked from one to the other, his eyes filled with compassion.

'It's the old ticker, Karel. The heart is like a fickle clock. You will have to slow down and work less. I'll give you pills for angina, but, if the symptoms persist, I'll have to send you for further tests in the hospital in Rheedershoek, which has a large heart unit and is the closest town to Malansdorp.' His own heart twisted with the inadequacy of his words.

Panic stirred in Miemie. She looked dazed while she absorbed the doctor's prognosis.

'Doc,' said Karel, leaning on the desk, 'in a few months I will cast a vote for the first time in my own country and Elizabeth will be coming home. It's this knowledge that will keep me out of the hospital.' He sat back, folding his arms defiantly.

Doc Joe nodded and stepped around the desk. He explained the care procedure to Miemie and handed her a packet containing the necessary medication. As they rose to leave, he placed a hand on the backs of both Miemie and Karel, guiding them to the door.

'Take good care of your husband, Miemie. He's a good man.'

They left holding hands, Karel leaning heavily on Miemie.

CHAPTER 32

LONDON

In St. James's Park in the heart of London, pelicans perched on branches of fig and Tibetan cherry trees. Cautiously, they viewed groups of picnickers on the lawns. Swans glided gracefully between waterlilies on lakes shimmering like mirages in the early morning light. Overhead, cormorants, coots and moorhens arced in formation across a cloudless sky. The outline of Buckingham Palace with its famous balcony towered majestically above the foliage.

Summer was unfurling; it was a flawless day.

Armed with a picnic basket, Robert and Elizabeth strolled across the verdant green lawn. She wore a white pinafore dress that hung loosely on her slender frame. Her long dark hair, in which silvery strands were beginning to appear, was twisted into a knot and pinned beneath a wide-brimmed hat.

Paul, Kiara, David and Anna had laid out rugs and set up chairs beside the lake in readiness for the planned picnic. Catching sight of Robert and Elizabeth, they beckoned to them, and they joined the group.

Kiara leaned against the back of the chair she rested in, cradling the dome of her belly. Pregnancy had rounded her cheeks and lent a glow to her skin. Paul and Kiara had decided on late parenthood. When Kiara's bump became visible, they announced triumphantly that the baby was a boy. 'We will name him Menachem Vihaan after both our grandfathers – Menachem being my grandfather's name and Vihaan is Kiara's grandfather's name.'

Paul had grinned boyishly, his glasses misting when he shared the joyful news with his friends.

They gathered around a low wooden table. Thick slices of freshly baked bread, wedges of cheese and servings of potato salad were placed on paper plates, still-warm apple pie was the treat.

Sitting cross-legged on the rug surrounded by the camaraderie and chitchat of the group, Elizabeth experienced the same flutter of happiness that had persisted since the news of the 'yes' referendum. Apartheid would be abolished, and she and Robert would be going home to South Africa. They would be reunited with their daughter who had been torn from her arms when still a baby.

And yet.

The fragile veneer of her happiness was splintered by flashbacks to the night she had left her baby behind in Zelda's care. Time had not obliterated the memory of the baby's warmth against her breast, her deep, rhythmical breathing, and her powdery smell. Would she bond with her adolescent daughter who was now a stranger? These questions haunted her.

The carefree conversation of close friends seated around the picnic table didn't veil what was uppermost in their minds. Robert turned to Paul and Kiara speaking earnestly, 'David and I are about to sell our law practice. Once the deal is concluded, Elizabeth and I will leave London. We plan to be in Cape Town for the election which, it is rumoured, will be in the first half of next year. Thabu and Sipho are preparing for our arrival and are helping me rent a suitable cottage in Rondebosch close to the university Emmy will be attending.'

David added, 'Anna and I are leaving within weeks. We want to enroll our daughters in universities before the beginning of the year. Now, at last, we will have a choice.'

A heavy silence followed David's words. Anna was lost in a fog of memories.

Kiara prodded her. 'You'll still be in London for the birth of Menachem. Besides, the three of us will visit South Africa now that Paul and I are considered legal.' She giggled mischievously.

The warmth of the day and the affinity of friends created a feeling of peace.

No one could have predicted the events that were yet to come.

Nancy and Elizabeth were enjoying a late breakfast in Reader's Nook.

Nancy had eventually decided to sell the shop and was laying out plans for her retirement to an attentive Elizabeth. The new owners of the shop were a young couple who appreciated her years of experience and needed her guidance. She would continue to live in her flatlet at the back of the shop. With a sideways glance at Elizabeth, she said, 'I intend to visit you in South Africa often.' Her statement elicited a hug from a tearful Elizabeth.

The shrill ring of the telephone cut across their conversation. Nancy stretched across the counter to lift the receiver.

'Hello Robert,' she smiled and passed it to Elizabeth. With the receiver cradled beneath her chin, Elizabeth inhaled deeply, her eyes widening as she listened to Robert's message across the airwaves. At the end of the call, she sat for a moment with the phone still in her hand, aware of a feeling of foreboding. Her lips quivered when she replaced the receiver.

'It's Karel, my father. Robert got a message from home informing us that he's not well and is receiving cardiac treatment. Although he's recovering, I'm anxious to go home immediately. Fortunately, the sale of Robert's practice is about to be concluded.'

'I'll miss you. You've been a daughter to me.' Nancy's voice was gruff with emotion.

The loud chiming of the doorbell that announced the arrival of a customer ended their conversation.

CHAPTER 33

TWEEFONTEIN

O nce the 'yes' referendum became a reality, the atmosphere bristled with anticipation of change. South Africans drew a collective breath as they waited for the date of the election to be announced. It would be the first time all races took part. Observers predicted that only a bloody revolution could overturn the brutally controlled regime. The white population, expecting the worst, stocked up on candles and canned goods, preparing to cloister themselves in the safety of their homes.

In the homestead on Tweefontein, the sitting room – *die voorkamer* – was flooded with sunlight. Zelda, her hair tied back in an unusually tight knot, sat on the blue velvet of a wing-backed chair gazing through the window. Dirk, sitting across from her, held a newspaper up to the light. His glasses had slipped to the end of his nose as he studied the headlines. His jaw jutted out. Concern furrowed his brow.

Outside, a fresh breeze had picked up, whirling the fallen oak leaves in circles around the stoep and against the window pane. Pietman Latief, armed with a rake, attempted to gather them into a large raffia basket. The acorns crunched beneath his sandals.

Turning from the window, Zelda caught her reflection in the glass panel of the stately grandfather clock. Though blurred, the vertical lines at the side of her mouth and feathery wrinkles around her eyes could not be masked. The years of activism and fighting for change had taken their toll. The imminent change in government would bring closure, and bring justice for her husband Dan. She shut her eyes, allowing his image to fill her vision.

In the dining room, Freda was preparing tea. A cake, frosted in chocolate, rested in the centre of the table. On a tray was a rose-patterned porcelain tea set. Stooping to place a teacup on the table beside Dirk, she scanned the headlines of the paper. Zelda watched them exchange a look, a silent fleeting glance. The government they had been a part of was bound to fall. A new dispensation, one they could never have imagined, would take its place. The look they exchanged was tinged with fear.

Freda handed a teacup to Zelda. The slight tremor of her hands caused it to rattle against the saucer. She, too, was not unmarked by the passing years. Her sloping cheeks were framed by hair blanched with age.

Dirk placed the newspaper across his thighs. He removed his glasses and rubbed his eyes with the heels of his hands and looked up. 'I have received the doctor's report on Karel's health. The prognosis is not good. His heart is irreversibly damaged, but Doc Joe will examine him regularly. Now that he no longer drives tractors on the farm, he spends his time leisurely at home. Miemie is a good nurse and will continue to attend to his needs.'

Zelda stirred her tea thoughtfully. 'It'll be a race for Elizabeth to get home before it's too late. Barney received a message that Robert and Elizabeth intend leaving London within the next few weeks. Their security in South Africa is still uncertain, but Karel's ill health has hastened their decision.' She added, 'Their arrival will be another upheaval for Emmy.'

The crunch of footsteps on the pathway was accompanied by a sing-song 'hello-o.' Emmy had spotted Zelda's Datsun in the driveway. On entering the room, her eyes lit up and she embraced Zelda, greeting Freda and Dirk enthusiastically. Lured by the chocolate cake, she raised a questioning eyebrow at Freda pointing to the remaining slices. Freda answered with a quick nod and waved her towards the tea table. Emmy took a generous slice and sat cross-legged on the carpet, licking the chocolate off her fingers. Zelda marvelled at how Emmy had emerged from childhood into adolescence. She had grown tall and lean and moved with the grace of a young foal. Gone were the pigtails and ribbons, now her hair hung loosely about her shoulders. She radiated an energy that filled the room.

Emmy delighted them with tales of her school-day escapades. They laughed a lot. It felt good. Then she became pensive and brushed the crumbs off her hands, her eyes searching each of theirs. 'When will my parents be returning?'

The abrupt question hung heavy in the air, followed by a long, simmering hush. Zelda saw the same fiery light of Robert's eyes in Emmy's. She felt her throat contract, making her unable to answer the question.

Dirk rose and straightened up, rubbing his lower back with both hands. He broke the silence, choosing his words carefully. 'We're expecting them to return within a few weeks. Barney will keep us informed of their intentions.'

Zelda studied Emmy's reaction, but her face was inscrutable.

Emmy glanced at the grandfather clock. 'I need to prepare Pa's dinner,' she said tonelessly, jumping up. Though she had left the room, her presence was still felt.

To his ears, Dirk's reply had sounded thin, but there was no definite answer to Emmy's question.

CHAPTER 34

LONDON

Menachem Vihaan, swaddled in a fringed white prayer shawl, lay cradled in his father's arms. It was the eighth day since his birth. A white skullcap dwarfed his tiny head and contrasted with his honey-coloured skin, silky dark hair and thick lashes that swept his soft cheeks.

Paul's smile broadened. It was part pride, part relief that the circumcision ceremony was concluded. Kiara was seated at his side. She had twisted her dark hair into a knot and pinned it on top of her head. Her loose-fitting white cotton dress gave her an ethereal appearance. The concern that had masked her face before the ceremony was replaced with a glow that lit up her large eyes. She cast attentive glances at the baby as she fussed over him, stroking his downy head.

The Rabbi walked over to Paul and Kiara. The attractive young woman had a prayer shawl draped around her shoulders, which partly covered her light-blue dress. A skullcap rested on her unruly auburn hair and her pale cheeks were dusted with freckles. She stroked her palm tenderly across Menachem's forehead and held her ringless hands above his head. She intoned a blessing and prayed that he would be a source of joy to his parents. Guests were milling about and they raised their glasses to a chorus of *l'chaim* – to life. Good wishes were repeated amid handshakes and hugs.

The Rabbi – 'call me Aviva' – drew up a wooden stool in the centre of the room. She perched on it, resting one foot on the bottom rung, and raised a guitar across her chest. There was a hushed silence as her melodic voice rose, gently at first, until it filled the room.

'How many roads must a man walk down.' She crooned the words of Bob Dylan, charming her audience. Swaying in unison, they joined the chorus, lustily singing, 'The answer my friend is blowing in the wind . . .'

Robert and Elizabeth were among the guests gathered around a trestle table that groaned under the weight of platters filled with delicacies. They delighted in the jovial atmosphere. The sun had dipped below the horizon when Aviva packed away her guitar and greeted each guest as they made their way home.

When the last guests had left, Robert approached Paul. His shoulders were slumped inside his tweed sports jacket, and the knot of his tie pulled askew. 'Bro, this is goodbye,' he said and clapped Paul affectionately on the arm. He added, solemnly, 'Elizabeth and I are leaving next week. We're following David and Anna who've already arrived back in South Africa. I'll continue working with our comrades in Cape Town to prepare for the election.' The breath snagged in his throat and he smiled wanly. 'I look forward to introducing you to Emmy when you visit.'

He glanced down at the baby, asleep in a cot at Paul's feet. 'You have a beautiful son. I eagerly anticipate watching him grow to manhood.' His voice quavered with emotion.

'Friend, allow me to drive you and Elizabeth to the airport when you leave.'

'I've arranged for a pool car to be delivered to the apartment in the morning. The same company will collect it at the airport once we leave.' Robert's smile and his arm thrown loosely around his friend's shoulder conveyed his appreciation of Paul's offer.

He was unaware of the magnitude of his decision.

Kiara and Elizabeth strolled arm in arm towards the men. Elizabeth stretched out her hands to grasp one each of Paul and

Kiara's. She was caught up in a combination of emotions. 'Your friendship has been a refuge for Robert and me. It has helped us get through the turmoil of our lives here in London.'

Gulping down a sob, she embraced Kiara one last time before she and Robert turned to leave.

Once outside, Robert impulsively turned the handle of the door, pushing it ajar, and retraced his steps. His gaze lingered on the vision of Paul and Kiara holding their baby, their heads bowed together. Sensing his presence, Paul looked up, but Robert had turned away and the door swung closed behind him.

It was this image of Robert and the haunting words of Bob Dylan's song, 'Blowing in the Wind' that would remain in Paul's memory long after Menachem had reached adulthood.

CHAPTER 35

Click clack, click clack, Elizabeth's footsteps reverberate on the bare floorboards and echo off the walls of the empty apartment. Crates filled with memorabilia of the long and painful years in exile are stacked in the centre of the room. She feels detached from the space that she and Robert had called home, now devoid of all traces of their daily rituals.

She sits on a crate and crosses her legs. Her elbow rests on her knee, her chin on her palm. She is surprised by the nostalgia that engulfs her, but it does not ease the regret for the years spent without her daughter. A sense of timelessness drifts between the walls of the apartment.

Robert joins her. He has been packing a travel bag in the bedroom and slings it across his shoulder. He eases the strap, running a thumb and forefinger beneath it. Elizabeth looks up at him for a long moment. Their eyes meet. Dreams and passion collide, and emotions are laid bare. Robert extends a hand to her: 'Ready?'

She nods and, rising, takes his hand.

A thread of trepidation trembles down Elizabeth's spine.

The squeal of tyres in the street below draws Robert's attention. Cupping his hands on either side of his face, he peers through the window. The sleek black vehicle from the carpool is parked beside the pavement. The driver stands in front of the car, feet apart, facing the window. He is dangling a set of keys which he holds up. Behind the parked car a rider straddles a motorcycle.

'It's time to leave, Libby.' Holding her hand, he guides her towards the door and they step outside. Robert turns to lock the apartment door. He removes the bag from his shoulder while he rattles the key until it clicks firmly into place.

Finally, they are leaving London.

Robert greets the driver who hands over the keys and then climbs onto the pinion of the motorcycle. The cyclist revs forcefully and together with his passenger sets off on the bike that roars around the corner and out of sight. About to open the car door, Robert stops mid stride, his face scrunched in agitation.

'Libby, I left my travel bag on the landing when I locked the door. Please collect it while I reverse the car.'

It was the stillness she remembered most. The apocalypse that enveloped her in a shroud of silence. Nothing moved. She felt elevated above the scene being enacted on the ground beneath her. Impassively, she stared at the flames shooting from the car when the bomb, triggered by the ignition key, exploded – and the shards of glass scattered in the street from surrounding windows. She did not hear the screams of passers-by or her own screams. The strap of Robert's travel bag bit into her shoulder, but she did not feel it. Amid the debris of suitcases torn apart by the blast, she recognised the shredded sleeve of the jacket Robert was wearing.

She closed her eyes wishing for oblivion, and allowed herself to slide into a dark tunnel of nothingness.

The explosion was heard many blocks away and into the heart of London. Sirens rent the air as ambulances and police cars cut through the traffic, blue lights flashing. Within minutes, the news of the car bomb reached Paul and Kiara. Numb with shock they rushed to Elizabeth's aid.

In the long days that followed, Elizabeth floated in and out of consciousness, her dull eyes barely registering her surroundings. Paul and Kiara had secreted her into their home, away from the prying eyes of the public, and away from the journalists hounding her. Kiara attended to her as tenderly as she did to Menachem. She washed and brushed her hair and coaxed her to eat. Nothing could draw Elizabeth out of the black abyss into which she had sunk.

'Be patient,' the doctor advised. 'Trauma has paralysed her. In time she will come to terms with her loss.' He placed his hand on Elizabeth's forehead and smoothed back her hair. 'Poor child, her suffering is immense,' he said, snapping closed his black medical bag.

His words proved prophetic.

After a restless night with a fretful Menachem, Kiara prepared breakfast for Elizabeth hoping to tempt her with freshly baked pancakes and cream. Still in her dressing gown and slippers, she carried the tray to the room and elbowed the door ajar. She gasped with astonishment.

Elizabeth sat in a chair beside the bed in which she had lain prone over the past days. She had brushed her hair and gathered it with a clip in the nape of her neck. The dullness in her eyes had disappeared. 'Who did this to Robert?' she said, looking pleadingly at Kiara who placed the breakfast tray on a table beside her.

'A far-right conservative party has claimed responsibility. Robert has been on their hit list for some time.'

Kiara sat facing Elizabeth. Thoughts shadowed her eyes. She put her hands on her knees and, leaning forward, spoke solemnly. 'War has the power to dehumanise people. Whoever did this to Robert was reduced by war to a monster. In all wars, we are intent on fighting for what we believe. We think it's all-important to achieve our ideals, but it is not. Nothing is more important than to maintain our humanity.'

Only then did tears flow. Elizabeth released her grief in great heaving gulps; the pain rising in waves as she wept in Kiara's arms.

Emotionally depleted, she looked up at Kiara. 'I need to go home. My father's not well, and Emmy is expecting me. As soon as I sort out my affairs in London, I'll leave for South Africa.' With Kiara beside her, their friendship unwavering, Elizabeth tucked ravenously into the breakfast prepared for her.

A flame shone defiantly in her eyes.

CHAPTER 36

TWEEFONTEIN

The media screeched the headlines: Robert Booth well-known communist killed in London in a car bomb.

The news of Robert's death filtered through to Tweefontein and the town of Malansdorp, sending shockwaves throughout the small community.

The farmworkers reeled at the news. They gathered around television sets and hungrily scanned newspapers to try to make sense of the horrific turn of events. Robert and Elizabeth's imminent arrival back on the farm had been widely anticipated, now there was no information about Elizabeth's whereabouts or whether she would be coming home. Rumours abounded.

'I said no good would come of Elizabeth Apollos's friendship with that Englishman,' announced Katie Plaatjies to a group huddled around a transistor radio. She folded her arms firmly across her ample chest and pressed her lips tightly together.

Within hours, reporters besieged the town. Their investigations established Elizabeth's background and her relationship with Robert. 'The Elizabeth Apollos Story' was the scoop they fought each other for. 'When is she coming home?' was the question most frequently asked around the town and on the farm by journalists, but the workers remained tight-lipped.

Dirk Coetzee had been the first to receive the news of Robert's death in a car bomb. Contacts from his political party alerted him.

The first call started a chain of events that would forever change many of the lives of Tweefontein.

The phone in the farmhouse rang incessantly as reporters hounded Dirk for information.

'No comment,' he said once again, replacing the receiver. Glancing out of the window, he drew in his breath – 'Freda, close the curtains!' he called in alarm. A group of reporters were converging at the farm gate.

With the house darkened, Dirk and Freda slipped out of the back door and made their way to the Apollos cottage. They aimed to break the news gently to them and to assure them of Elizabeth's safety.

Zelda and Barney heard of the tragic event in a telephone call from Dirk. Consumed with shock and grief, they headed for the farm. They bypassed reporters at the gate and sped along the gravel road towards the cottage. Zelda clapped the palm of her hand onto her forehead and emitted a low moan at the scene they encountered. The car shuddered when she braked suddenly, the wheels spinning in the gravel.

An ambulance was parked at the gate and the front door of the cottage was thrown wide open. Raised voices were heard coming from inside. Doc Joe was directing four white-clothed medics carrying a stretcher. Karel lay prone on it, a monitor attached to his chest.

Dirk was assisting the medics carry the stretcher into the back of the ambulance. A distraught Miemie and Emmy followed behind the medics.

'Wh-what happened?' Zelda's breath caught in her throat.

Doc Joe answered, his expression grave. 'Karel has suffered a heart attack. He needs to get to the hospital. Every minute counts.'

Zelda drew herself up to her full height and took control of the situation. 'Climb into my car,' she instructed Miemie and Emmy, gesturing with her head. 'We'll follow the ambulance to the hospital.'

Miemie and Emmy clung to each other in the back seat of the speeding car. Gulping down her tears, Miemie relayed the events of the past few hours.

Dirk and Freda had arrived at the cottage and gently informed them of Robert's death. Karel and Miemie, staring straight ahead in stunned silence, had absorbed the fact that Elizabeth would not yet be coming home. Emmy would not be meeting her mother and now she would never know the father she had longed for throughout her childhood. A pall of grief had descended on the hushed room, broken only when Karel emitted an anguished cry and, with a thud, fell to the floor. Emmy and Miemie's cries had alerted the farm workers in the nearby fields, who dropped their tools and rushed to call for the doctor.

Zelda sped behind the ambulance with its blaring sirens. In the stressful race against time, Miemie stole frequent glances at her wristwatch. The minutes ticked slowly by. Then the hospital loomed into view.

Throughout the day, Miemie and Emmy sat at Karel's bedside. As night advanced, the world outside felt dark and silent.

Nurses, radiating kindness, slipped in and out of the ward, the rubber soles of their shoes squeaking on the linoleum floor. Deftly, they adjusted the tubes attached to Karel and competently monitored his heart rhythm, glancing sporadically up at the overhead machines. Miemie and Emmy were plied with sandwiches and hot drinks. The nursing staff urged them to return home, but Miemie and Emmy were adamant in their refusal and curled up for the night in armchairs beside Karel's bed.

Emmy fell into an exhausted sleep, her head resting on her arms, her hair spilling down the side of the chair. *The child needs rest*, and Miemie covered her with a light blanket provided by the nurses.

The overhead nightlights were turned on, casting the ward in a harsh glare. The floor had been mopped at the end of the day and the acrid smell of disinfectant clung to the air.

Miemie sat rigidly watching over a motionless Karel, the slight rise and fall of his chest was the only sign that he breathed. Her eyes never wavered from him. She observed how the years had taken their toll; the gnarled and spotted hands that lay folded beneath the sheet and his bony shoulders covered by the grey hospital gown. Just for a moment, she screwed up her eyes tightly, trying to reconcile this gaunt figure with that of Karel, the boy with the gentle brown eyes who had once spilled a drink down her Sunday dress at a Christmas party.

In the still of night, when the only sound was the wheeze and splutter of instruments in the ward, shadowy ghosts from the past invaded her reverie, unspooling the years of her life. Images of Elizabeth, who had chosen a path that took her far from home and family, mingled with those of Emmy. The cruellest of fates had now left the child fatherless.

She rubbed a hand across her eyes.

Painful, deeply buried memories began effortlessly to emerge.

The house on Victoria Street lay on the outskirts of Malansdorp, where the coloured folk lived. The corner plot on which the house was built was larger than the others on the block. A spreading fig tree, heavy with fruit in the summer months, shaded the front garden. All year round, glass jars filled with fig jam and compote lined the pantry shelves. Unlike the other kids in the neighbourhood, Ousis and Miemie had a bedroom to themselves while Ma and Pa slept in a separate room.

Miemie considered herself fortunate. Ma didn't clean houses like most of the other mothers, but she took in mending occasionally. She spent most of her days at home and was always there to greet her and Ousis with a hot meal when they returned from the farm school.

The little luxuries of their lives were made possible because Pa held a job at the government offices in the town. He was clever and had a way with figures. She felt proud when he was promoted to the position of manager of his department.

She loved Pa. When she struggled with maths, Pa made it seem easy and when she achieved good marks he placed shiny pennies in the palm of her hand. With the pennies, she was able to purchase bags of Wilson toffees and Chappies bubblegum at Connie's Corner Café.

In the evenings, when Ma did her mending Miemie sat cross-legged on the floor beside her, handing her pins and thread.

'Why is Pa's skin lighter than yours and mine?' she asked Ma, with the lamplight illuminating the questions in her eyes.

'Pa's father, Oupa Leo, is German and Pa inherited his fair skin.'

Miemie became thoughtful, absorbing the information. Persistently, she queried, 'Why don't Oupa Leo and Ouma Elsie ever come to visit us at the same time?'

Ma gave a long, exasperated sigh. 'They were married before apartheid became the law of our country. Now, because Elsie is coloured, it is dangerous for them to be seen together. They could be jailed for many years just for living together.'

Then, playfully, she swatted Miemie's head. 'No more questions tonight, child.' She packed away her mending and turned down the light.

The day disaster struck the Baartman family, rain clouds had been gathering ominously, shrouding the town in a gloomy light.

He wore a khaki uniform with a baton attached at the waist. The peak of his cap shaded his small, calculating brown eyes and beaklike nose. His name was Wynand Brits and he was from the Department of Home Affairs. 'I have been instructed to test you, to decide which race you belong to,' he smirked, producing a sharpened pencil which he threaded into Pa's woolly hair. It did not fall out.

'Ah ha!' gloated the officer triumphantly. 'That proves you are a coloured man. You have been earning a white man's salary. Your pension will be cancelled, and you are dismissed immediately from this office.'

The Baartman's lives were shattered. It seemed to Miemie that overnight Pa withered. Gone were the shiny pennies for treats.

Stoically, Ma took control of the situation. Ousis and Miemie were taken out of school and sent to work as housemaids. Ma increased the mending she took in, adding washing and ironing. Pa was diminished. Humiliation and injustice caused him to descend into a dark place. He never again left the house until the day he gently closed his eyes and passed into oblivion. When the doctor was asked for the cause of death, he shrugged his shoulders, helplessly.

'I guess he died of a broken heart.'

The laboured sound of Karel's breathing roused her from her reverie. Gazing at his motionless figure she was overwhelmed with tenderness and felt a need to take his hand. She pulled it from beneath the covers and squeezed his fingers. He turned his face towards her, recognition flickering in his watery eyes. His dry, flaky lips moved slowly: 'I can see Libby asleep on the chair. I knew she would come.'

Miemie nodded, aware that he believed Emmy was Elizabeth. He grunted contentedly before the light in his eyes faded and he turned his head away.

The unbroken beep of the monitor sent the young doctor scuttling to Karel's bedside. He glanced at the instruments and turned sorrowful eyes to Miemie. He raised his shoulders, his lips pulled tight. Miemie leaned across the bed and pressed her mouth onto Karel's cold forehead until the nurse gently pulled her away. Miemie turned to Emmy sleeping in the chair and encircled her in her arms. She whispered her out of sleep.

'Pa's gone.'

Only two words were spoken, the rest were left unsaid.

CHAPTER 37

LONDON

Autumn in London was brief but glorious. Sunlight spilled across a cloudless sky burnishing the foliage to shades of crimson and gold. Light frost in the early morning, however, was a harbinger of the long, cold winter about to arrive.

As days turned to weeks, Elizabeth grappled with the reality of all she had lost. Kiara provided solace when grief threatened to overwhelm her. Paul assisted with intricate legalities, the consequences of the bomb blast that killed Robert.

But it was Rabbi Aviva's frequent visits and her aura of warmth and empathy that helped to bring Elizabeth the peace that had eluded her. Aviva's keen perception of Elizabeth's mixed emotions, her anger and frustration, helped Elizabeth to regain her composure and, with it, her feistiness. In a twist of fate, she would be returning to her home, her parents and her daughter, but without Robert.

It was the arrival of Anita, Kiara's mother from Calcutta, that brought a sensation of joyfulness. She swept into the house enveloped in a silver and magenta sari, lifting the veil of despondency that had hovered over the Weiss household since Robert's violent death. Her hooped gold earrings dangled noisily whenever she spoke, which she did often and animatedly. She cradled Menachem and he slept peacefully in the folds of her silken sari, no longer fretful. Anita demanded that Kiara rest. Paneer tikka masala bubbled on the stove, the tempting aroma floating throughout the house.

When Anita was introduced to Elizabeth, she studied her, tipping her head this way and that. She sensed her pent-up tension. 'Elizabeth, I can't change the past, but I can help bring tranquillity back into your life.'

Later that day, soft pillows were placed on the floor. Elizabeth followed Anita's example and settled cross-legged onto one. She circled her thumb and forefinger and rested her wrists on her knees.

'Now close your eyes and take a deep breath.'

'Aum – aum –' Elizabeth echoed the older woman's chant, her shoulders slumping as the tension eased from her.

In this way, a ritual of meditation began for Elizabeth, one that she would follow for all her life.

Anita was preparing rotis in the warm and cozy kitchen. Elizabeth watched in awe as she deftly folded each one, smoothing the edges.

Paul appeared at the kitchen door. Elizabeth looked up in surprise. 'Paul,' she exclaimed, 'why are you home so early . . .?' Her voice trailed off in midsentence. Seeing the severity on his face, her breath caught. Stony-faced, Paul handed her a folded page and she sat down on the kitchen stool. Moving to the edge, she pressed her elbows on her knees and unfolded the page: Karel Apollos passed away peacefully last night.

Her eyes glazed over; her lids fluttered. Then she buried her head in her hands and wept. Paul and Anita stood by helplessly as she poured out her grief in gulping sobs. Through a blur of tears, Elizabeth looked up.

'I must go home now. Ma needs me.'

The memory of Anita, her warm rotis and inspirational meditation, would linger with Elizabeth long after she had left London and the warmth of the Weiss family for her home in South Africa.

PART THREE

CHAPTER 38

TWEEFONTEIN

Ma's appearance at the cemetery sends a shudder of recognition coiling down Elizabeth's spine. She seems withered, her rheumy eyes tinged with yellow, her white hair cropped close to her skull. Elizabeth takes Ma's outstretched hands into her own. They are as dry and veined as autumn leaves and she lays them against her cheek. Her tears spill through fingers that are knotted with arthritis. Ma lifts Elizabeth's chin and searches her face, but offers little in the way of talk.

Hand in hand, the two women set out on the dusty gravel path leading up the hill to the cottage with golden pumpkins on its roof. Memories abound, strengthening the bond of mother and daughter. The years apart stretch between them. Words are superfluous.

Behind farm cottage windowpanes myriad eyes follow their journey. The observers understand that this moment of the long-awaited homecoming belongs to Miemie, Elizabeth and Emmy alone. High up in the oak trees, children sit on branches with their legs dangling down and watch in wonderment as the women make their way along the path – Miemie, shrunken and stooped, beside her beautiful and wilful daughter. A sense of awe engulfs Tweefontein.

Emmy waits expectantly at the cottage gate. Elizabeth blinks as her eyes rest on her daughter. She stands stock still. Emmy appears carved out of the sunlight that surrounds her. Hesitantly, Elizabeth takes a step towards the girl. In that moment, layers of time peel back revealing an aching throb of yearning. She gazes into her daughter's eyes and gasps, covering her mouth with her hand.

Emmy will never know how closely she resembles her father, she thinks as Robert's piercing blue eyes look back at her – the curve of his eyebrow, his lopsided smile. 'Robert,' she murmurs, 'this is your daughter.'

Conflicting emotions cross Emmy's face. She tosses her fair hair back over her shoulder, then places her hand on her thrust hip.

'Welcome home, Elizabeth,' she says laconically and turns away.

CHAPTER 39

The afternoon sun filters through the window of the homestead kitchen bathing it in a warm glow. Fine particles of dust dance in the bright light. There is an ageless quality to the kitchen.

Elizabeth and Zelda are seated at the wooden table in the middle of the room. Freda stands with her back to them, gazing through the window. She appears thoughtful as she slowly stirs a mug of coffee, releasing its aroma. The percolator burbling on the stove is the only sound.

Elizabeth's elbows are placed on the table her palms propping up her chin. Her eyes are downcast. Her slumped shoulders and the stillness that surrounds her give her a defeated look. Opposite her, Zelda pages listlessly through the newspaper without reading it. Zelda has recently acquired wire-rimmed spectacles. She removes them and wipes the lenses, using a methodical circular motion, before replacing them. She rises with slow purposeful movements and lifts the percolator from the hob, filling two mugs with the steaming liquid and handling one to Elizabeth.

The women's presence provides Elizabeth with a safe and trusting space. She needs to confide in them. 'She treats me like an intruder,' she wails, breaking the silence. 'I feel like a guest invading the space between her and Ma. I can't win her over.'

Freda turns away from the window and gives a tired smile. 'Libby you will have to be patient a while longer. Emmy carries so much unresolved pain inside her. She's a strong girl but needs time to adjust to you. She's still grieving for Karel. There are many issues for her yet to work through.'

Zelda interjects. Her expression is wistful. 'The general election is almost upon us. Karel wanted so much to be part of it and Robert sacrificed his life for a change in government. Both have been denied their right to vote for change.' For a moment, her strong façade crumbles and she appears vulnerable. She bites her bottom lip. Her words hang heavy between them.

Elizabeth attempts to lighten the atmosphere and lifts her head, squaring her shoulders. She addresses the women with a proud note in her voice. 'Before he was assassinated, Robert rented an apartment close to UCT where Emmy is enrolled. She's eager to start classes. Ma and I will relocate with Emmy once her school term is over.'

In the far corner of the kitchen, Katie Plaatjies is ironing, her back and shoulders curve over the ironing board. She lays a dampened cloth across the garments before sliding the hot copper iron over them. The cloth hisses and steams. She pants with exertion. Snippets of conversation have been drifting towards her. Aware that Miemie is being discussed, she places the iron upright and strides up to the women. She folds her arms beneath her apron and blows out her cheeks before she speaks. 'Miemie's not the same person she was before Karel's death. She's not well.' She presses her lips together. Smiling enigmatically, she turns and walks back to the ironing board.

Katie's words register unspoken fears. A silent glance passes among the women, and they move closer around the table.

'She's become forgetful,' Elizabeth acknowledges softly. 'She appears to be living in the past, imagining that Pa is still with her. Doc Joe has prescribed medication, but she is fragile.'

A loud banging at the kitchen door distracts the women. Pietman appears in the open doorway. '*Goeie dag* – good day,' he calls, smiling broadly and revealing the space that his front teeth once occupied. 'Where shall I put the Christmas tree?' he asks, directing his question to Freda. He holds out the large box he carries. 'I've got decorations and fairy lights to put around the farm in time for the New Year's Eve party.'

'The Christmas tree should be put in the front room,' says Freda, with a wave of her hand. Pietman disappears behind the kitchen door.

At the mention of Christmas, a shadow crosses Elizabeth's face. 'Soon it'll be Emmy's birthday,' she murmurs. There is a stillness in her mind, a lingering sensation. She gets up and paces slowly, chewing thoughtfully at a thumbnail. Abruptly, she returns to her seat and faces Zelda and Freda. She stretches her arms across the table, clasping their hands.

'I have Robert's bag,' she confides. 'It's the one he left on the landing, the one I went back to fetch before the bomb detonated. It contains a batch of letters addressed to Emmy. Unbeknown to me, on each of her birthdays he wrote her a letter detailing events in our lives before we left for London, and those in the years we lived in London. In them, he expressed his deepest emotions – his love for her, his sadness at leaving her behind and his longing to be reunited. He intended to hand them to her when we arrived back home.' Her voice is thick with emotion and she lowers her head.

When she looks up, memories have softened her eyes. 'Now I'm going to hand them over to her on her birthday. I hope that Robert's letters will help her reconcile with the past and accept the events that have brought us to this moment.'

Freda and Zelda nod enthusiastically. Hope is etched on their faces. Each woman bears witness to the vestiges of a past life.

CHAPTER 40

A chorus of birdsong stirred the residents of Tweefontein into wakefulness. Downy rays of the sun dissolved the night's shadows.

Emmy's bedroom door was ajar. Elizabeth peered around it hesitantly.

The girl lay sprawled on the bed, her hands behind her head, her ankles crossed. She was wearing pink shortie pyjamas and fluffy pink slippers.

She looks more like the little girl she sometimes is, and not like the sophisticated teenager she wishes to be, thought Elizabeth.

'Happy birthday, Sweetheart,' she called.

Emmy blew a strand of hair away from her face and turned to the wall. Elizabeth swallowed nervously and pushed the door wide open. She patted the cover on which Emmy lay. 'May I sit down?'

Emmy shrugged, detached, her face still turned away.

Elizabeth attempted a smile. 'Zelda has invited us to spend your birthday at her home. Barney will also join us. I'm told this is a tradition.'

'My class is having a slumber party at Marie's house tonight and I plan on spending the day with her. Besides Oumie is not well and I need to be here to help her,' Emmy answered petulantly.

'Emmy, where are you child – *waar is jy kind?*' Oumie called from her bed. She was propped up on pillows. There was a vague expression in her eyes. Emmy swung her legs off the side of the bed and gathered her hair into a band in the nape of her neck.

'Coming Oumie, I'll bring your tea.'

Alarm clouded Elizabeth's eyes. *She thinks of Emmy as her daughter and has forgotten about me. She becomes more confused with each passing day.*

Elizabeth followed Emmy to the kitchen. The girl stood with her back to the door, rattling the cups.

'Turn around, Emmy. I need to give you something.' A hard note had crept into Elizabeth's voice, one that Emmy had not heard before. Surprised, she swung around to face Elizabeth. Her eyes fell on Robert's travel bag on the table. She raised her eyebrows questioningly, her lips parted as though to speak.

Elizabeth unzipped the bag and removed a bundle of letters tied up with faded ribbon. She walked over to Emmy and put the bundle into her palms. Placing her hands on Emmy's shoulders, she looked deeply into her daughter's eyes and spoke intensely. 'These letters are a precious gift from your father. Read them carefully. The last letter is the one he intended to hand to you himself. They are all I have of him to give to you.'

Then she turned abruptly and walked away.

Emmy watched her mother leave. Her face crumpled; her veneer slowly cracking. She wiped her forearm across tear-filled eyes and stood rooted, feeling utterly alone. She stared at the pile of letters and was caught in a mesh of emotion.

How I shall miss Zelda and Barney today. It's not true that I have plans with Marie and now there's no turning back. The painful thoughts caused her stomach to cramp.

'Emmy!' Oumie's strident call summoned her and broke into her dejected reverie. She put the letters back on the table and carried Oumie's tea and a buttermilk rusk to the bed where she lay. Oumie nodded her appreciation and looked up at the girl through milky eyes.

'Pa's coming to have tea with me,' she sighed happily.

Emmy sat on the bed beside her. *When did her hair become so white?* she wondered, as she gently stroked Oumie's creased forehead.

'Pa is no longer with us,' Emmy murmured gently, but Oumie had a dreamy look and seemed not to hear. She lifted the cup to her lips with trembling hands. When Oumie had drained the cup, she closed her eyes.

Emmy lowered her head into her hands and her shoulders heaved with silent sobs. Oumie was drifting away from her and Pa's death had left her with a constant ache. The father she had yearned for would forever be just a phantom-like figure and now she had alienated her mother. Loss overwhelmed her. She lost track of time while she sat beside Oumie listening to her fractured breathing.

She sensed a presence behind her and turned around. Elizabeth stood in the doorway illuminated by the morning light. She gazed at her daughter's tear-stained face and held her hand out to her.

'It's not too late. The bus leaves for the town in the next hour. You'll be back in time for the slumber party tonight. Katie's daughter, Rachel, has offered to watch over Oumie until we return.'

The girl's thoughts were in turmoil. Her mother had abandoned her and she had learned to live without her. But now that Elizabeth was home Emmy acknowledged that she needed her. She wanted her to stay. Something shifted inside her and, in that moment, her reservations began to crumble.

She took Elizabeth's outstretched hand.

CHAPTER 41

Days had passed since Elizabeth had handed Robert's letters to Emmy but they remained unread. The unopened envelopes lay on a table beside her bed.

The night was drawing in. Emmy lay on the couch, listlessly paging through a school textbook. Elizabeth was curled up in a chair. Her thoughts raced. She observed how the house displayed its age. Cracks like spiderwebs had appeared in the walls now that Pa was no longer around to fix them.

All her attempts to draw Emmy out had failed. The girl was reluctant to read Robert's letters. She was morose, answering in monosyllables. Elizabeth's frown deepened. She was acutely aware that the contents of the letters would unleash a torrent of emotions. *Is Emmy prepared?* Robert had been meticulous in recounting the past. She tapped a forefinger against her lips evaluating the situation before quickly making a decision. She rose and crossed the room to where the letters lay.

'I'll sit next to you while you read these,' she said, handing the letters, still tied together, to Emmy. She nudged her daughter and moved up close to her on the couch. Emmy turned to face Elizabeth, the sullen set of her face softening. Tentatively, Emmy tugged at the faded ribbon until it parted and the letters cascaded about her. Elizabeth nodded encouragingly and squeezed her hand.

Oumie's wheezing breath drifting in from the bedroom was the only sound as Emmy immersed herself in each letter written to her by her father. The tip of her tongue poked through the side of her mouth as she concentrated. As the hours passed, the look that swept across her face was at times dark and sober but occasionally she giggled and nodded in recognition of an event Robert described, and turned to Elizabeth for confirmation. They read the letters together, Emmy instinctively shifting closer to Elizabeth.

It was past midnight before all the envelopes had been opened and lay scattered about, some having slid onto the floor. All but the last one. Still unread, it lay in Emmy's lap.

This was Robert's last letter to her – her only connection to a father she'd never known.

A ribbon was tied around the letter. Emmy undid it and held the envelope in her hand as though trying to weigh it. Then, hesitantly, she lifted it, studying it at arm's length. Her name was scrawled across it in her father's now-familiar script. Her eyes were cloudy with confusion. She was struggling to absorb the thoughts and emotions that Robert's letters laid bare. In his scrawling handwriting, she had followed her parents' journey; their yearning for home; their hopes and fears for their child; the ache of longing and loneliness; and their courage in enduring the unbearable burden thrust upon them. She reeled from the revelations that were unbalancing her fragile world.

Elizabeth nodded reassuringly to Emmy, who still held the unopened envelope. Then she broke the seal. The pages fluttered down and she unfolded them. She placed her elbows on her knees and, leaning forward, she began to read.

My dearest daughter,

This is my last letter to you and will be the shortest. There will be no need for another as we will be together to celebrate your next birthday.

My child, how I long for that moment. In my dreams I watch you run towards me on a sandy beach, and I swing you up into my arms. I see your beautiful face wreathed in sunshine.

But that is my dream, not yours.

It is my wish that you will reach for your dreams. You were never meant to fulfill mine but, in some way, you have allowed me to let go of dreams I was never destined to fulfill.

Although you were torn away from your mother and me in circumstances we could not control, we never relinquished you but carried you with us in our hearts. Our unwavering belief that we would be reunited with you enabled us to carry on; it programmed us to move forward.

Emmy, you will live your life in a free country with all the good that your mother and I and others fought so hard to achieve. Like us, never give up on your goals.

I have come to believe that freedom is in your mind and it is only your thoughts that imprison you.

It was my choice to live a perilous life and, although my future is still uncertain, it is a choice I have not regretted.

My love, if the choices I made have wounded you, that was never what I intended. Forgive me, my only intention was to love you.

I shall always be beside you.

Your father

Robert Booth.

Somewhere in the distance, a clock struck the hour. The sky was beginning to lighten. After peppering Elizabeth with questions, Emmy's eyelids drooped and she yawned deeply while gathering up the letters. Mother and daughter made their separate ways to bed, to spend what was left of the night. Unseen by Elizabeth, and before sleep claimed her, a tear slid down Emmy's cheek which she wiped away with the flat of her hand. Alone, she would weep for all that she had lost and could never regain.

It was a glorious late summer afternoon. The sun beat down relentlessly on the house on Magnolia Street. Elizabeth, Barney and Emmy were sheltering from the heat in the shade of the stoep overlooking a rose garden. The open blooms created a colourful carpet, their delicate perfume drifting in the air. The gentle hum of bees seeking nectar added to the tranquillity of the scene.

Zelda was preparing lunch in the kitchen and the rattling of cutlery and crockery mingled with their conversation. Lunch would be served when Thabu and Sipho arrived to join them.

'We plan to relocate to our apartment in Rondebosch within a few weeks,' said Elizabeth, speaking over her shoulder to include Zelda in the conversation. Barney waved a newspaper to cool the air and rearranged his bulk in the chair, attempting to find relief from the heat. He nodded approvingly at Elizabeth's statement.

'Ma is stubborn,' continued Elizabeth. 'She's refusing to leave the cottage on Tweefontein and is adamant that she will not live with me and Emmy in the apartment. But,' she added, wistfully, 'the cottage is showing its age. Cracks and fissures are appearing. Without Pa to fix it . . .' she ended, abruptly blinking away tears. She tried to summon Pa's face but saw instead a broken image on a splintered mirror.

Zelda stood at the kitchen stove. Overhearing the conversation, she turned around, brandishing the spatula she was using to stir. 'Miemie may be stubborn but she is reasonable. She cannot stay on her own in the cottage. Now that she owns it, arrangements can be made with Dirk Junior to sell it. She'll take time to adjust to new surroundings, but will have Emmy and Elizabeth's support.'

The discussion ended when the sound of laughter at the back door announced the arrival of Sipho and Thabu. Sipho wrapped Zelda in a hug and waved a brown-paper bag in the air. 'I've brought pastries,' he said proudly. 'And after the election, we won't have to slip in through the back entrance.'

'And I won't have to wear a chauffeur's uniform,' added Thabu, laughing. He discarded his jacket, perspiration beading his forehead.

Despite their merriment, a pall of uncertainty settled over the group. South Africans of all races were torn apart by fear of political violence and by divisions within their communities. With Nelson Mandela's release from prison, a change of government was certain – the writing was on the wall.

When they had gathered around the table, Zelda set out platters of sizzling fried snoek, garlic rolls and an assortment of salads, the tempting smell teasing their nostrils.

The conversation turned to Emmy.

She seemed to radiate a contentment they had not seen before. Zelda and Barney revelled in the newfound happiness of their young prodigy. They sensed, however, that although Elizabeth's arrival had provided a measure of stability for Emmy, challenges still lay ahead. Alone, in the quiet moments of contented friendship, they marvelled at the impact the girl had had on their lives.

Zelda and Barney locked eyes across the table, reading each other's thoughts. Memories of Robert passed painfully between them. He had come so close to realising his dream of a free

South Africa and being reunited with his daughter. Silently they acknowledged that, like the consistency of the stars, Robert's light would forever shine.

The sun had slipped over the horizon when Elizabeth rose to leave. She hugged Sipho and Thabu. 'Rachel has been caring for Ma today but now I must return.' She held out a hand to Emmy gesturing for her to follow.

Barney jumped up, displaying some of his old agility. His eyes swept over the group. 'I'll be meeting you at the voting booth next month.' His statement was acknowledged with nods and handshakes, but there was a lingering unease as they parted.

'I do hope Miemie adapts to the move,' Zelda ventured to no one in particular. Her brow was puckered with uncertainty.

Then Elizabeth and Emmy climbed into the car for the drive back to the farm.

Midnight bestowed its magic on Tweefontein as day dissolved into night. Somewhere in the eerie silence, a night owl hooted. Threads of moonlight trailed across an inky sky. The town seemed otherworldly, adrift in a sea of shadows.

The occupants of the cottage on the hillock close to the stream slept soundly.

Then Miemie began to toss restlessly.

'I want to stay in the cottage with you, Karel,' she murmured drowsily. 'Don't let them take me away to live in the city.'

Karel appeared at her bedside.

'I knew you would come, Karel,' she whispered. With her hands flat on the bed, she pushed herself up to face him. He was encircled in a halo of light.

'Dance with me, my love,' he said, extending both his hands.

Miemie swung her legs off the side of the bed. She looked down and was surprised to see that the green dress with the white ruffles around the neckline had replaced her night dress. She laughed aloud when Karel slid the matching slide into her hair. He folded his arms around her, and she lay her cheek against his chest.

He danced her across the room. Then he whirled her around until her feet lifted off the ground.

Hand in hand, eyes locked, they danced in unison, whirling up into the sky amidst a galaxy of dazzling stars. Higher and higher they floated until he danced her off the edge of the world.

They found her the next morning in the milky light of day. She was slumped on the side of the bed, enveloped in an aura of serenity. Her journey on earth was complete.

A mound of new earth beside Karel's grave told their story. It was a tender love story, one of steadfast devotion, and an immutable bond between two lovers as united in death as they were in life.

PART FOUR
EMMY'S STORY

CHAPTER 42

When Elizabeth and I moved into the apartment in Rondebosch, it indicated a new beginning.

Losing Oumie so soon after Pa shattered my world. Oumie had been the fierce protector of my childhood; she and Pa had provided me with a measure of stability. I carried my grief silently in my heart.

Elizabeth's arrival had caused another upheaval in my life but, after so much loss, I could not lose her too. I wanted to salvage our fractured relationship. A storm of emotions swept through me and I drifted in its wake.

Dirk and Gerda Coetzee had become too frail to run the farm. Before we left it was sold to an American investor. Katie Plaatjies, Pietman Latief and the other loyal farmworkers shared in the profit. The Apollos cottage and the land on which it stood were part of the deal. The funds Elizabeth received went towards my university fees. A torrent of tears was shed by the entire community on Tweefontein when the Coetzees relocated to live with Dirkie and his family in Johannesburg. It was the end of an era for the line of Coetzees who had tilled the soil of Tweefontein.

The moment we left the farm, it was as though a door slammed shut on my childhood. But my memories will always persist and will not be eradicated by time. They will always be a part of me.

My destiny, it seems, has been shaped by decisions others have made for me.

Zelda still lives in the house on Magnolia Street and my childhood bedroom remains untouched. It is a cocoon of familiarity when I visit her. I speak to Zelda, addressing my fears. She is an insatiable reader and has a spiritual philosophy. Her words are reassuring.

'Your mother didn't dwell on her regrets and neither should you. Heaven knows she has enough to regret.' She gazes thoughtfully into the distance and then turns back to me. 'The one thing she has never regretted is giving birth to you.'

Zelda has lost none of her vigour. The gatherings in her house with Barney, Thabu and Sipho are among my most enduring memories.

Unbidden, an admiration for Elizabeth is creeping up on me. She is smart, decisive and has a steely determination which has enabled her to find employment in a legal firm, Mendel Moodley & Associates. She will be Mister Mendel's assistant. Each morning, she leaves for the city in the blue second-hand Toyota she recently purchased. When she returns in the evening, we prepare dinner together and eat it on our balcony. We watch the stars in their constellations in an indigo sky. Only when the moon crests the mountaintops do we retire to bed.

I was beginning to feel as though the balance of my life was being restored.

Then came my first day at university and my initiation into drama school. I had taken a year off to deal with my grief and to settle into our new surroundings before registering for my course. With mounting excitement, the day finally arrived.

The morning dawned bright and clear. A few wispy clouds, harbingers of rain, curled lazily around Signal Hill. I stood on the balcony, pensively watching a flock of birds fly in perfect formation into the pale light.

It was Freshers Week. Throughout the week, new students are introduced to their lecturers and each other. I pulsed with nervous excitement. My school friends had drifted off, pursuing their chosen careers. Marie, my best friend, remained in Malansdorp where she had secured a position as a teller at the local bank. Her friendship bolstered my confidence, and I felt lost without her at my side. The fear of making new friends made my stomach clench.

Elizabeth and Zelda had carefully selected outfits from the department stores in the city to replace the dungarees and tracksuits I wore on the farm.

I dressed carefully that first morning, choosing a pink floral ankle-length skirt and white button-up shirt. I brushed my hair until it shone, then I gathered it in the nape of my neck and braided it into one long plait that hung down my back.

Walking into the kitchen, I found Elizabeth there preparing breakfast. The aroma of freshly scrambled eggs and warm blueberry muffins drifted towards me, tempting me, but anxiety curbed my appetite. I pushed aside the plate she set before me. She urged me to try a muffin dripping with butter. I did, then asked for another. Sensing my trepidation, she hugged me reassuringly before she left for the office. I stood on the balcony, this time watching her speed off in the blue Toyota.

It was a short bus ride to the University of Cape Town. The imposing building was built in a classical revival style. Steeped in history, it rises tall and stately against the backdrop of Table Mountain. Groups of students had gathered on the steps leading to the portal and they chatted animatedly to each other or lounged beside their tog bags.

I climbed the steep steps, following the signs to the office where a tall middle-aged woman with sloping shoulders stood checking the register. She smiled kindly, asked my name, and waved me into the lecture hall. I followed the raised voices of the clusters of students standing in the aisle.

A glance at the group caused me to freeze. I registered dully that, in my long floral skirt and with my hair braided, I looked nothing like them. I didn't fit in. The girls were uniformly dressed in blue jeans and loose-fitting T-shirts, their long hair cascading about their shoulders. Most wore make-up. Summoning up the courage I did not feel, I entered the room and took a seat in the back row, trying to make myself small.

At the end of the speech of welcome to us students, I hesitantly approached a group of girls and introduced myself. 'Hi,' I ventured, addressing the tallest one. 'My name's Emmy Booth. Which course have you enrolled for?'

'Drama,' she answered brusquely. The girls exchanged silent looks that spoke volumes, and then they sauntered away. Tears pricked my eyes. I slipped the sling of my satchel over my head and slunk off the campus, heading back home.

My heart was heavy. I longed for the security of Tweefontein. I yearned for Oumie and Pa. I sat at the kitchen table, my chin in my palms and my eyes downcast.

'Hello-o, I'm home,' Elizabeth called and entered the apartment at the end of her working day. She took a step back when she sensed my dejected mood. Her brow furrowed and her eyes clouded with concern.

'Why do you look so gloomy?'

I lowered my head in my hands and wept with disappointment and frustration. Elizabeth remained stony-faced and stood calmly by, listening to my rendition of the day's events. Then she turned around, busying herself preparing a mug of hot chocolate and a peanut butter sandwich, guessing that I had not eaten lunch.

'Tomorrow will be different,' she soothed, placing the warm mug in my palms. But her words felt empty and did little to pacify me. I went to bed consumed with anger and hurt. It took a while to sleep, but eventually I slipped into a strange slumber and dreamed of Oumie, Pa and Ousis.

I awoke the next morning with a sensation of dread. I weighed up my choices. Should I face the other students again or stay under the duvet for the day? I slipped my arms into Oumie's old dressing gown and slouched into the kitchen.

Elizabeth was nowhere to be seen. I called her name but there was no reply. Peeking around her bedroom door, I noticed her bed neatly made as though she hadn't slept there the night before. Confused and concerned, I returned to the kitchen to prepare breakfast. Then I caught sight of a note propped up against the kettle. It had my name scrawled across it in her handwriting. I turned it over. 'Back Soon' was all it said.

When I heard her key scrape in the latch, I ignored the cooling tea and marmite toast I'd prepared. The door burst open before I could reach it and Elizabeth stood framed in the entrance. She was laden with varied-sized shopping bags that were emblazoned with well-known designer logos. She smiled a curious half-smile and gestured with her chin for me to follow her to the full-length mirror in her bedroom.

'Now let's get you ready for Freshers Week.' She gave a satisfied grin.

I was breathless as she withdrew denim jeans and an assortment of T-shirts and beaded sandals from the bags, arranging them on the bed for my inspection. Hastily discarding Oumie's dressing gown, I pulled the jeans up over my hips and slipped my feet into the sandals. Wide-eyed, I observed my transformation as I twirled around in front of the mirror. Then she brushed my hair over my shoulders and trimmed a fringe across my forehead.

'I'll be late for work, and you'll be late for lectures if we don't hurry,' she chuckled. I stared at my image in the mirror, enthralled with my new look.

Before leaving, she turned back at the door and retraced her steps. 'I almost forgot to give this to you.' She searched in her handbag and handed me a silver vial of pale-pink lipstick. 'Have a good day,' she called, blowing me a kiss.

I felt a surge of love for the enigmatic woman I had not yet called mother. She tugged at a corner of my heart, which I had thought was permanently closed.

I was adjusting to life as a drama student and to the thrumming of campus life. Elizabeth and I were settling into a rhythm, becoming accustomed to the fast pace of city life. Lectures, study and socialising left little time for anything else. My visits to Zelda and Barney dwindled. Elizabeth worked long hours, often bringing work home to complete in the evenings. Mister Mendel was becoming more dependent on her. Streaks of grey shot through her ebony hair. Against her cinnamon skin, it added to her beauty. I was proud to introduce Elizabeth to my new group of friends. We studied together in the evenings and the girls in the residences visited the apartment over weekends.

On the university grounds, the leaves on the trees, and on the ivy that clung to the surrounding walls, were turning to orange and gold. Traditionally, this was a signal for students to begin preparing for the coming examinations. I immersed myself in study, determined to be successful.

I was in the canteen between lectures when my newly acquired mobile phone alerted me. Zelda's name popped up on the screen. Guilt pricked at me. It was weeks since I'd last spoken to her.

'Zelda I'm so sorry . . .' my words came out in a rush.

'I am aware that it's exam time, Emmy.' Zelda's familiar gravelly voice came calmly back. 'But I've missed you and it's Barney's birthday next week. We're celebrating at a restaurant in town and he wants you and Elizabeth to join us. Will you come?'

'We will,' I accepted, enthusiastically. After a more innocuous conversation, I thanked her for calling and flipped the phone cover, ending the call.

Hurrying along the corridors to the lecture theatre, I was suddenly catapulted to a different time and place. My conversation with Zelda had triggered a long-buried memory.

In my reverie, I am a child again. It's my seventh birthday. I leave with Zelda in her Datsun and the pain of Oumie and Pa being left behind is as acute now as it was so many years ago. I remember Zelda's attempts to pacify me, to explain gently that we are unable to celebrate together in a 'whites only' restaurant because of the colour of their skin – because Oumie and Pa are brown. I gulp down a sob.

The elections have come and gone. South Africans from all walks of life have embraced the new dispensation in our rainbow nation. No longer are restaurants and public spaces reserved for white citizens only. We have witnessed Nelson Mandela, holding hands with his wife Winnie, march triumphantly out of the gates of prison. With Zelda, Barney, Thabu and Sipho, Elizabeth and

I were among the hordes of Capetonians standing shoulder to shoulder on the Grand Parade. We waited with bated breath for Mandela to deliver his iconic speech from the balcony of the City Hall. Crowds cheered, they pushed and screamed, craning to catch a glimpse of the future. The final curtain was about to fall on the horror of apartheid.

I feel my chest constrict when I remember that Oumie, Pa and my father Robert did not live to be part of a free South Africa.

I am startled when students jostle me along the corridor, eager to be seated in the lecture hall and I am reeled back to the present.

CHAPTER 43

Jenny is tall and statuesque. She has flaming red hair and a personality to match.

Although she was among the group of girls I had attempted to befriend on that unhappy first day of Freshers Week, we are being drawn to each other and a tenuous friendship is forming. We enjoy spending our lunch hour together in the canteen and slowly discover that we have a lot in common. I no longer feel rejected and alone. I am honing my talent in class under the keen eye of the lecturer and beginning to recognize the feeling of being happy.

Jenny invites me home on a Saturday evening. Elizabeth and Mister Mendel, or Max as she now refers to him, have been spending time together after office hours. Saturday night will be such an occasion, so I don't feel guilty accepting Jenny's invitation.

Her family's home in Camps Bay is situated on the slopes of the mountain. It is brightly lit when we arrive in the early evening and we stand on the balcony to watch the rolling waves crash on the pristine white beach below. Eventually a full moon hovers above palm trees that line the wide road. The view leaves me breathless. I am intimidated. Her home is so different from any I had known in Tweefontein.

Shyly I introduce myself to her parents, Simon and Olga Gelb. They are effusive in their welcome and I instantly warm to them.

We are seated around a dinner table and Jenny's three siblings join us. Two are twin boys and the third a younger sister. They all have the same red hair, which is inherited from Simon who sports an auburn goatee and is otherwise bald.

'Eat, eat, my child,' Simon coaxes as platters of succulent grilled fish and side dishes are brought to the table.

The conversation around the table is rowdy and at times difficult to follow. The boys vie with each other to be heard above the din and Simon gives a throaty laugh whenever something is said that amuses him. Jenny gives me a look of exasperation and mouths 'Don't mind the boys' but I am fascinated by this exuberant family. I enjoy their company as well as the delicious food that I sample, and hope that the meal won't end soon. I revel in their warmth.

Olga Gelb is a small retiring woman who doesn't say much but smiles a lot. She taps a fork against the side of a glass. The boys become quiet and all eyes turn to her. 'Desert will be served. It is Pavlova and ice cream,' she announces. This makes the boys whoop loudly and argue about who should get the first scoop. The chaotic meal ends with promises extracted from me to return.

The evening has given me a peak into a family so different from my fragmented one, but which I am beginning to feel part of.

Like a butterfly emerging from a chrysalis, I feel a metamorphosis occurring within me.

Jenny owned a yellow Mini and was, therefore, the envy of other students – most of whom walked or caught buses. At times a few of us would club together to fill the petrol tank and pile into the car to be ferried between campuses.

After the Saturday evening dinner with her family, Jenny drove me home.

Arriving at the apartment in Rondebosch, I was elated to see lights burning. I tingled in anticipation of recounting the events of the evening to Elizabeth. When I entered the apartment, I heard a clatter of crockery and followed the sound into the kitchen. Elizabeth was at the table buttering mounds of bread in preparation for a picnic planned for the following day. Her eyes lit up when she saw me and I dropped into a chair beside her. She handed me a knife and gestured towards the butter.

She noticed my flushed face, put down the knife and cocked her head, a quizzical expression on her face. 'Seems you had a good time,' she said.

Although it was almost midnight, I was pumped with excitement and eager to share details of my evening with Jenny's family. While we prepared the sandwiches together, Elizabeth listened attentively. She laughed at my childlike wonder before she waved me off to bed and cleaned up the kitchen. The sound of her laughter felt good to me. It wasn't a sound I had heard often, not since I'd left the farm. She was mostly moody and preoccupied. There was a haunted look in her eyes and I knew that her thoughts were filled with memories of Robert. At times she would hold up a picture of him to the light, anguish contorting her features. Her sighs seem to emerge from somewhere deep inside her.

'You are so much like him,' she declared, emotion cracking her voice and I wondered if I was a reminder of all she had lost.

At moments like those, I was tempted to reach out and hold her in my arms; hold the broken parts of her together, but a persistent voice in my head prevented me. 'She abandoned you,' the whisperings echoed around me.

Still, we were subliminally slipping into the roles of mother and daughter.

The Moses family – David, Anna and their daughters – joined us the next day for the picnic we'd planned on Muizenberg Beach. The family were frequent visitors to our home, lifting Elizabeth's spirits whenever we spent time together. Our shared pasts bonded us as closely as a family.

David, through years of working with Robert, was able to fill in details, creating an image of my father that grew ever more real, providing me simultaneously with a history and a future. At times, the stories he told had me crying with laughter until I realised that my tears of mirth were mixed with those of sorrow.

How can I miss someone I never knew?' I brooded while Robert's image grew larger and more significant in my world.

Our extended family, which now included Max Mendel, was growing and with it my sense of security.

CHAPTER 44

It all happened in a week, one in which it felt as though my world had tilted on its axis.

Final-year drama students were producing plays for their year-end exams. Jenny and I were given roles in a play by Frederico Garcia Lorca, entitled *Blood Wedding*. I had a minor role as the bride's maid, but I embraced it. Rehearsals were scheduled to begin immediately.

The creaking wooden floor of the stage, the musty smell of the heavy curtain, and the sticky stage make-up became part of my world. I was consumed by the theatre and revelled in its ambiance. Slipping into the role of my character made me feel as if I were living a childhood dream. Rehearsals were long and exhausting, but I gave up my time effortlessly because on stage was where I felt most comfortable.

It was the end of another long session of rehearsals and the cast had striven for perfection. Opening night was looming and our excitement mounting. I was alone in the dressing room tissuing off the grease paint when the door flew open and Jenny rushed in, still in full costume and make-up.

'Hey, Emmy,' she said, excitedly nudging me with her elbow. 'My cousin Eden and his friends have invited me to join them for cocktails in Camps Bay. Do come along.'

'Another time, Jen,' I answered, yawning deeply. 'I'm worn out after rehearsals today. Besides, Elizabeth is expecting me for dinner.'

'Aw, come on Em,' Jenny coaxed. 'Call Elizabeth from my phone and let her know that you'll be home later.'

I did. And that was when my universe changed course.

Summer, shrugging off the last of winter, had emerged into a sun-soaked world. It was dusk. The yellow Mini sped along the mountain road high above the Atlantic coastline. Jenny was at the wheel. I craned my neck to stare out of the window, awed by the spectacle below. Uninterrupted powdery beaches shimmered against the turquoise hues of the sea, while white-capped waves foamed onto the water's edge.

Yet a feeling of unease persisted. In my mind's eye, I saw Elizabeth dining alone on the balcony. Guilt washed over me. Besides, I was uncomfortable when meeting strangers. Jenny's city-bred friends intimidated me. I mulled over the foolhardiness of my decision to tag along.

Sensing my mood, Jenny cast a sidelong glance at me. 'Why so glum, Em?'

'Just tired, I s'pose.' I yawned, then stretched and folded my arms behind my head.

'Fresh air will revive you,' Jenny declared. She rolled down the window and the salty sea air rushed in, whipping through my hair. Jenny's chatter and the cool air lifted my spirits, as she had predicted.

The sky was darkening when we arrived at Camps Bay. The setting rays of the sun brushed the sky into a burnt-orange sunset. The pavements were thronged with pleasure seekers. Laughter, loud music and honking traffic vied with the crashing waves and cawing of seagulls. We threaded our way through the crowds towards the designated restaurant.

'There they are,' Jenny bumped her shoulder against me, waving at a group of young men seated at a table conversing animatedly. The tallest one rose, beckoning to us.

'That's Eden,' she mouthed as I followed her.

'Hi, I'm Frankie,' said a fair-haired member of the group and extended a hand. I gauged him to be my age. The friendly faces around the table put me at ease and I felt my apprehension ebb. Much later, Eden signalled to a waiter and ordered a round of burgers and hot chips. I had not yet eaten and hadn't realised how hungry I was. Once the waiter had removed the empty plates, Eden swung his chair around to face me.

Eden Gelb was olive-skinned with dark hair that curled over the collar of his blue open-necked shirt. Stubble darkened his jawline. He straddled the seat, folding his arms across the backrest, and leaned closer to me. I was aware of the intensity of his heavily lashed green eyes.

'Tell me about yourself, Emmy Booth.'

At ease in his company, I related anecdotes of my childhood on the farm. At times he would frown bemusedly but my descriptions of Pietman Latief and Katie Plaatjies had him laughing out loud. He had an irresistible laugh which got me giggling, until we were both laughing so hard that we gasped for air.

Wiping my eyes, I tilted my head to the side raising an eyebrow questioningly at him. 'Now tell me about yourself.'

Eden nodded and moved his chair closer to mine. He began to relate his story.

During the apartheid years, his father, unable to come to terms with the government's laws, left South Africa and settled down on a kibbutz in Israel. It was there that his father and mother met. They married while on the kibbutz, which is where he and his younger brother Doron were born. The family returned to South Africa once apartheid was finally abolished.

I was engrossed in Eden's story and was listening raptly when Jenny tapped her foot against mine under the table, startling me. Glancing at my watch, I realised how much time had passed. 'Oh-oh,' I exhaled, covering my mouth with my hand, and jumped up. After hasty goodbyes, Jenny and I headed off to the car.

I was drawn to Eden, experiencing feelings I had not felt before. Secretly, I hoped we would meet again.

The Mini's headlights pierced the night as we headed back to the suburbs. 'You seem to have got on well with Eden,' Jenny said, smiling cryptically.

I felt a flush of heat, but shrugged nonchalantly, staring out of the window at the darkened streets. Seeing the window reflect my expression, I hoped it hadn't betrayed my secret thoughts.

Days passed since our visit to Camps Bay and, although I had been drawn to him, Eden had not attempted to contact me. Each morning, I searched Jenny's face hopefully. If she was aware of my hankering to meet him, she showed no sign of it. No invitation from Eden was forthcoming.

To hide my disappointment, I threw myself into rehearsals, volunteering to help backstage. It kept me working late into the evenings and I often got home after dark.

The frenetic days filled with lectures and rehearsals had Elizabeth and I passing each other like ships in the night. Breakfasts were rushed, eaten standing in the kitchen while catching up on the previous day's events. I would hear her Toyota revving as she left for work. Most evenings she returned after I had turned out the light.

I was captivated by the transformation I observed in Elizabeth. She spent hours at the beauty parlour and had her hair styled into a fashionable bob. Purchases from city boutiques filled shopping bags stacked in her bedroom, the contents spilling out of them.

'Do you like it?' I was preparing for bed when she stood at my bedroom door, hands on her waist and her hip thrust out. Then she whirled around.

I nodded and held my breath. The ruby-red dress was belted and had a wide flared skirt. It was unlike anything I had seen her wear before. The sensible straight skirts and button-up shirts she wore for work were relegated to the back of her wardrobe.

Max Mendel was the catalyst for the change in Elizabeth. He had begun to play an important role in her life and was steadily slipped into mine.

The sun had barely risen when the shrill ring of my alarm clock jolted me awake, reminding me of an early tutorial. The rattling sounds of crockery coming from the kitchen and the waft of fresh coffee confirmed that Elizabeth was preparing breakfast.

When I entered the kitchen, the smell of burnt toast filled my nostrils. Sheepishly, Elizabeth held up a slice of blackened bread.

'Not again. This time I'll watch the toast while you scramble the eggs,' I said with mock exasperation, popping two slices of bread into the toaster.

She stood at the stove with her back to me. 'Em-mee,' she said plaintively over her shoulder, and then she turned to face me, holding the spatula aloft. 'Max has invited both of us to dinner at his home tomorrow night. Will you come?' Her words came out in a rush. She gazed at me biting her lower lip. I heard the tremor in her voice.

Her question caught me off guard. I had not yet come to terms with many of the changes in my life. Although I was still unable to call her 'mother', Elizabeth and I were tentatively forming a relationship. Would Max come between us; did I even want him in my life? Emotions rolled over me in waves. Sensing her anxiety, I swallowed nervously before I answered, 'I will come' – although my expression conveyed 'maybe'.

She heaved a sigh of relief, and I watched the tension ebb out of her hunched shoulders. 'Shall I collect you after rehearsals tomorrow evening?' she said, looking directly at me. When I nodded, a smile lit up her face. She piled the scrambled eggs onto the freshly made toast and together we sat down to eat.

CHAPTER 45

It was sunset when we reached Max's home on the slope of Lion's Head. He welcomed us at the entrance wearing a striped butcher's apron, determined to display his cooking skills. Elizabeth and I perched on high bar stools in the immaculate white kitchen. We chopped salad greens into an enormous glass bowl while Max stood at the stove attending to a pan of trout sizzling in butter. The smell was enticing. My stomach growled, reminding me that I was hungry. My lunch, consisting of canteen sandwiches and tepid tea, had been consumed hours before.

Deftly Max plated the meal and we carried it out onto the balcony where a dinner table had been prepared. In the distance, palm fronds swayed across a sky dusted with stars. A panoramic view stretched to the endless horizon. Pleasure boats, their headlights glowing, chugged across the ocean and a passenger liner that was dressed in a rainbow of coloured lights lay far out to sea. I was enchanted. And the meal was delicious.

Until that moment, the conversation had been light-hearted. Max peppered me with questions about my course, and he listened closely to my answers and my aspirations, nodding occasionally or holding up a finger for me to elaborate on an answer.

A framed picture of a smiling young woman with a tangle of blonde curls caught my attention. It was an arresting photo with the woman gazing directly into the camera lens. 'Who is she?' I asked, frowning slightly.

He swallowed and peered into the distance as though seeing images that I could not. He shifted in his seat. When he looked back at me his face was filled with emotion and he exhaled as though to empty his lungs.

'Marilyn', he said softly, 'was my wife. She fell ill just before we married. She was a brave fighter. We both believed she would recover but it was not to be, and she died in the first year of our marriage. She was young and beautiful and had a passion for life. I still mourn her.' His eyes held their faraway look and his hands lay folded in his lap. Turning to face me directly, he continued. 'My life became meaningless, and I chose a solitary existence. Work was my refuge. Elizabeth', he said shyly, leaning across to take her hand, 'has brought a spark of light into my dark world.'

She held his gaze for a long moment, their exchanged looks revealed a lot, and then she slipped her arm through his. They both turned to gauge my reaction to their open display of affection.

I looked away, needing to corral my emotions. The pounding of waves far below was the only sound in the still night. My thoughts turned to the contents of Robert's letter.

Elizabeth was the recalcitrant daughter of Karel and Miemie Apollos. Beautiful and rebellious, she had gone in search of justice but instead had found love, for which she had paid a heavy price. But she carried her burden of loss with quiet dignity and grace. I could not deny her the peace she had found with Max.

I carefully threaded my words together. 'We have all suffered so much pain. It's time to heal. You've brought joy to Elizabeth, and so to me.'

There was an audible sigh of relief from both Max and Elizabeth.

But the spectre of Robert hung over me, woven into an endless tapestry of human frailty.

CHAPTER 46

Disaster struck three days before the opening night of *Blood Wedding*. Crystal, who took the leading role of the bride, came down with flu and her powerful voice was reduced to a croak. Then the stage manager dropped a set on his foot, splintering both the set and his foot. Chaos reigned.

Each cast member offered a remedy to restore Crystal's voice. Oumie's recipe of lemon and honey in a steaming brew of Rooibos tea proved most effective. The day before opening night, Crystal's rich voice once again filled the auditorium during rehearsals. A carpenter worked throughout the night to rebuild the set and Derick, the stage manager, appeared backstage again, hobbling in a plaster cast. Order was once more restored. Enthusiastically, we returned to rehearsals.

On opening night, the heightened atmosphere was charged with a mixture of excitement and trepidation. The rustle of patrons taking up their seats grew louder as the auditorium filled up. When the house lights dimmed, an expectant hush fell over the audience. The heavy velvet curtains swished apart and each cast member fell seamlessly into position.

The production ran smoothly and the audience was riveted. When the final curtain came down, the applause was tumultuous. I stood on the apron of the stage among the cast, taking a final bow. Surveying the sea of faces, my eyes fell on the second row. There, seated alongside each other, were Elizabeth, Max, Zelda,

Barney, Sipho, Thabu, David and Anna. A flush of joy warmed my cheeks when I looked at their beaming faces, filled with pride. Their presence conveyed a message of unconditional love and support.

For just a moment the audience faded away and I drifted, letting my thoughts reach into the past. Destiny had conspired to bring me to this moment and into the midst of a loving family. An image of Oumie and Pa elevated above the audience appeared to me until I blinked and it faded, but I still felt their presence.

The chattering of the audience leaving the theatre wrenched me from my musings.

My large extended family would be waiting to greet me in the foyer, and I would embrace them.

I lay in bed staring at the ceiling. I had decided to skip morning lectures. Tonight was the final performance of *Blood Wedding*. Elizabeth had left for the office and the flat was quiet. In the silence, my thoughts tangled like sea anemones twisting on the ocean floor.

Blood Wedding had been a resounding success, playing to a packed house on most nights. I embraced the experience. I was comfortable on stage. It reaffirmed my decision to choose acting as a career. Immersing myself in my character provided respite from the troubling thoughts that plagued me.

My hope that Eden would contact me after our brief encounter was slowly fading, yet disappointment gnawed at me. And I still harboured an undercurrent of resentment towards Elizabeth. If she had not left without me all those years ago, I would have known my father. The image of him that I conjured up was slowly dimming.

'You are so like him,' she repeated wistfully in answer to my queries. 'Look in the mirror and you will know Robert from your reflection.'

But, when I looked in the mirror, it was the eyes of a stranger that looked back at me.

The alarm clock buzzed on the table beside my bed and I glanced at the time. It was seven-thirty. I stretched my arms above my head. Throwing back the bedclothes, I swung my legs over the side. The day had just begun and I wanted to be part of it.

I dressed leisurely, then sat at the large ornate mirror that had once belonged to Freda Coetzee. I gathered my hair high onto my crown, secured it into a ponytail and then drew it over my shoulder, carefully brushing out the tangles. I studied my reflection. Eden occupied all my thoughts. Had I misjudged him? Was the connection I had felt just a figment of my imagination? Self-doubt consumed me and reminiscences of my first day at university haunted me. I felt utterly rejected.

Although I tried to push away his memory, it still intruded, unbidden, into my dreams and thoughts. I recalled the way his mouth curved and the candid gaze of his green eyes. Logic dictated that I should let go and forget about him, and yet I clung to a spark of hope that we would meet again.

In the kitchen, I poured myself a tumbler of fresh orange juice and leaned against the counter sipping the cool liquid. The silence felt oppressive and, abstractedly, I turned on the small transistor radio placed on the windowsill. The announcer's voice filled the room, breaking the silence.

'The Truth and Reconciliation Commission has been convened to expose the crimes of the apartheid area.' The voice droned on, followed by a discussion about South Africa's recent win in the World Rugby Cup. Nelson Mandela had worn a Springbok shirt and cap to hand over the trophy to Francois Pienaar.

Distracted, I was about to switch off the radio when the voice of a caller to the radio station drew my attention. I turned up the volume, riveted by the caller's recounting of a protest march.

'It was a day in September. I was part of a peaceful march of black students in Cape Town,' he recalled. 'The march occurred after the sixteenth of June protest march against the introduction of Afrikaans as a medium of instruction. The students were met with extreme police brutality on that September day. The march incited the police to loosen teargas over the city, causing mayhem. Shops and offices were closed and the traffic stopped. The following day, the police again used teargas and rubber bullets to disperse the crowds of demonstrators and onlookers. I was at the entrance to the Strand Street concourse when teargas was fired into it. All around me, people were collapsing. Because I was at the entrance, I managed to escape. However, two visiting All-Black rugby players, who were signing autographs, got caught up in it. The government was embarrassed.'

'Who won the rugby tournament?' interjected the radio announcer.

'South Africa,' was the triumphant answer.

This time I did switch off the radio and turned to rinse my tumbler, placing it upside down at the sink. A note propped against the kettle caught my eye. It read: 'Home late tonight. Don't wait up. Warm up the meal in the fridge. E.'

Her signature was a tacit acknowledgment that I did not call her 'mother'. Oumie occupied that space in my heart, and I ached with longing for her and Pa.

The cast had gathered in the canteen and I slid into a seat beside Jenny. They were in a celebratory mood and I soon got caught up in the playful rivalry and jest. We collapsed into uncontrollable giggles reminiscing about backstage blunders. My melancholic mood was lifting.

High windows in the canteen let in an abundance of light. Jenny prodded me, peering through the window. 'There's a cloth on the mountain,' she said, pointing to a heavy layer of white cloud tumbling over the mountaintop. Ominously, clouds were gathering momentum as they rolled down the side of Lion's Head.

'Oh no,' murmured Crystal, grimacing. 'If the wind picks up and develops into a black south-easter, we'll be playing to a half-empty house tonight.'

Jason, who played the part of the 'Groom', waved his phone in the air for attention. He relayed the message he'd received. His expression was grim. 'The weather bureau is predicting gale-force winds and hazardous weather conditions.'

His words were followed with a chorus of 'but the show must go on' amid laughter and merriment. Glasses were raised to a refrain of 'To Blood Wedding'.

The clouds kept rolling in.

It howls. It tears branches from trees and uproots saplings, trampling everything in its path. The ferocious wind known as the Cape Doctor gathers strength as it hurtles down the mountain slopes, releasing its fury on the earth below.

Backstage, we raise our voices to be heard above the sound of the wind whistling through cracks and crevices. It is minutes before the last call for us to take up our positions and we scramble onto the stage. I peek through a gap at the side of the curtain.

Empty seats stare back at me. Predictably, owing to the weather forecast last-minute cancellations are made and only a smattering of patrons occupy the theatre. Still, the cast members radiate an electric air of fervour. Our enthusiasm cannot be dampened.

Amid high fives and thumbs-ups, the curtain rises for the last time on *Blood Wedding*. The murmuring in the audience subsides. When the curtain finally falls on the last act they respond rapturously, rewarding the actors with a standing ovation. I am among the cast members standing in front of the footlights. We clasp hands, holding our arms up high in a gesture of appreciation. Then houselights flood the theatre and I peer out over the heads of the audience.

Eden is seated in the third row. He is beaming up at me. I feel my heart jump into my throat and for a moment I forget how to breathe. He catches my eye and I look back at him. He has not forgotten me. I am filled with joy. Rooted to the floor, I forget to move off stage when the curtain comes down. Jenny prods me and I stumble before regaining my composure and following the rest of the cast out.

Backstage, Jason opens a window in the dressing room. 'The wind has subsided. It seems to have blown itself out,' he says over his shoulder. A light breeze rustles the flimsy curtain at the open window. I close it and press my forehead against the cool glass, squeezing my eyes shut. Emotions rage within me.

'C'mon Emm,' Jenny beckons from the open door, her voice insistent. 'I'll be waiting for you in the foyer.'

Dabs of cold cream and tissues soon remove my make-up, and my stage costume is replaced by jeans and a pink T-shirt with the slogan 'If you think you can you can' printed across its front.

Eden and Jenny are waiting for me in the dimly lit foyer. Groups of actors are gathered around animatedly discussing the high and low points of the production. I walk towards Eden. He smooths back his hair and hunches his shoulders forward, his hands are in his jacket pockets. I have forgotten how tall he is.

'You were great,' he says, addressing both Jenny and me. He smiles and I notice the dimple in his chin. Then he reaches out as though to embrace me, but thinks better of it and pulls his arm back. I look into his eyes and feel I cannot look away. He seems to be reading my thoughts.

'I was at the opening night hoping to meet you after the performance, but you were surrounded by family members and I did not want to intrude.'

Unsaid words clog my throat and I swallow nervously. I am uncertain how to respond. My silence goes unnoticed. He quirks an eyebrow, 'Will you meet me tomorrow night at Dino's Diner? Come along too, Jenny – Frankie will be there.' We both nod enthusiastically.

Eden walks towards the door. Reaching it he turns and gives a mock bow. 'I hope that aspiring young actresses won't find the company of lowly accountants too boring,' he says with pretended seriousness. We all burst out laughing.

Then he is gone.

Together with the rest of the cast, Jenny and I leave the theatre.

CHAPTER 47

The year was drawing to a close. The gale-force winds that batter the city abated, ushering in summer. Hedonistic pleasure seekers thronged the sandy beaches or cooled their golden bodies in the azure Atlantic Ocean.

Lectures and exams were over for the year and I had, triumphantly, passed into the second year.

The high-ceilinged campus library was a cool refuge from the intense heat. Most of the students had left for the summer break and, other than Mrs Knox the librarian, I was alone at the table. The unfamiliar silence felt surreal. Mrs Knox had helped me select the required literature for my second year and the books were piled on the table. I ran my tongue along my upper lip, concentrating as I scribbled notes.

The constant hum of a nearby fan broke my concentration and I leaned back, chewing the end of my pencil. In the silence, I paged through my memory. I recalled events of the past year and my journey from a naïve farm girl to a self-assured, confident student, effortlessly merging with my peers. For a moment, I marvelled at my adaptation into a world so different from all I had known on Tweefontein.

But my memories of the little house on the hill beside the stream, in which I had spent my childhood with Oumie and Pa, had not dimmed. Nor had the raw grief that still assailed me at unexpected moments. My world on Tweefontein had been secure and predictable, but all that had changed when Elizabeth returned. I sighed, releasing tension. Unresolved resentment of Elizabeth still plagued me.

My musing was broken into by the vibration of my cell phone on the table. I flipped the cover, read the text message from Eden, and smiled. 'Meet me after work. Bring a bathing suit.' His messages were always short and to the point.

Since the closing night of *Blood Wedding*, Eden had added a new dimension to my world, and we drifted into a comfortable relationship. Jenny and Frankie had also linked up and, as a foursome, we enjoyed spending time together. Jenny and I would sunbathe between the brightly coloured huts on Muizenberg Beach while Eden and Frankie surfed, cresting the high white-capped waves. Eden introduced me to clubs and at night we danced to music pumping beneath coloured strobe lights. Elizabeth, sleepless, waited anxiously for me to return.

I was coming to accept my flimsy happiness.

Then came the call from Zelda.

Elizabeth was speaking into her cell phone while climbing up the stairs to our apartment. The worried look on her face made me fearful. 'Barney has had a heart attack. He has been released from hospital and is convalescing at Zelda's home.'

Within minutes we were in the Toyota and heading towards Magnolia Street.

'He looked so well last Sunday when we lunched together,' Elizabeth said, frowning as she navigated the traffic.

'There was an affinity between him and Max,' I added, nervously chewing at a thumbnail. In my mind's eye, I recalled the dash to the hospital when Pa had had a heart attack. As though reading my thoughts, Elizabeth said, 'Barney is expected to make a full recovery.' Then she swatted my hand to stop me chewing my nails. We both smiled and I gave a small sigh of relief.

Barney was resting on the couch with a rug across his knees. He smiled wanly. I struggled to conceal my shock at the change in him. His auburn tufts appeared whiter than before and even his belly was diminished. He held up his arms to embrace me and patted the couch beside him. I curled up, folding my legs beneath me, and threaded my arm through his, resting my head on his shoulder. My heart surged with love for the man who had played a defining role in my childhood and who had stoically stood beside me throughout my formative years. The smell of soap and familiar aftershave were strangely comforting and we sat that way until he grasped my chin and looked into my eyes.

'I have heard,' he said, with mock seriousness, 'that you have a boyfriend.'

'He's nice,' I answered snuggling closer to him.

'When will we meet him?' His voice was challenging.

My heart skipped a beat, his question made me swallow apprehensively. How would Eden react to Elizabeth and my racially mixed background? Or to the part played by my parents during the apartheid years? The questions tormented me. Apartheid was abolished and my group of friends reflected all skin tones but, at times, I sensed a simmering prejudice, evoking memories of the suffering inflicted on Oumie and Pa. I bit my lower lip and took a while before answering.

'Soon,' I said and hastily jumped up to help Zelda and Elizabeth prepare snacks in the kitchen, relieved to evade more questions.

Much later on the drive home I mulled over my conversation with Barney. Fear of revealing my heritage to Eden was a dark cloud that hung over me. I would have to confront it.

CHAPTER 48

The breeze picked up, whipping the waves into a white froth and leaving its salty residue on our skin. It was late afternoon. Eden and I strolled hand in hand along the Blouberg beachfront. Across the ocean, Table Mountain was superimposed on a brilliant sky. It formed a backdrop for surfers and bathers, for mothers pushing strollers, and for the elderly simply soaking up the sun on the crowded boulevard. Brightly coloured umbrellas fronting pavement cafés offered shade.

'This one,' announced Eden. With his hand on my back, he steered me towards a green-and-white striped umbrella. Sheltering from the sun and wind, I sank into a wide wrought-iron chair and stretched my legs. The waiter hovered until we had selected milkshakes from the many flavours offered on the plastic menu. I gasped at the size of the tall chocolate-filled glasses he brought to the table. Eden chuckled at my surprised expression and leaned across the table to smooth a wisp of windblown hair off my forehead.

'It's your birthday soon. What shall we do to celebrate?'

The question caught me off guard. 'Traditionally, I spend the day with Barney and Zelda.'

Eden raised an eyebrow and shrugged nonchalantly, but he looked disappointed.

I lowered my lids and drew in my bottom lip, my thoughts racing. Barney's request to meet Eden had struck terror into my heart. Eden knew so little about me. How would he react to my unconventional background, to Oumie and Pa, or to Elizabeth and Robert's activities during the apartheid years. These questions haunted me.

Having finished our drinks, we rose to leave.

Eden's question was left unanswered.

In the still of night, with sleep eluding me, I had devised a way to reveal my past to Eden, aware that I would have to accept the consequences.

We reached the crowded parking lot. Before climbing into the jeep, I turned to face him, my eyes burning into his. It was time to confront Eden's question.

'To celebrate my birthday, there's a place we need to visit. It's a fisherman's cottage on the coast near Simonstown,' I said earnestly, gauging his reaction.

He shrugged and turned his palms up. 'When?' he said, bewildered.

'Tomorrow.'

He patted my arm and gave my hand a reassuring squeeze. I felt my heart flutter with affection for him.

Now there was no turning back.

CHAPTER 49

The sun had barely risen when Eden and I headed out of the city. Simonstown was uncharacteristically cool for mid-summer. A fine mist hung over the sea. I shivered and hugged my satchel protectively against my chest.

We waited in the jeep until a weak sun filtered through the mist, revealing an unbroken expanse of white sand. Further up the beach, weathered, thatch-roofed cottages were dotted along a windblown grassy verge.

'I think it might be here,' I said, hesitantly, tenting my eyes and peering into the distance. From the scant details in Robert's letters, I was attempting to locate the hut he and Elizabeth had lived in while in hiding from the security police and before he had left for London and Elizabeth for the farm.

Eden's eyes glinted with intrigue.

'Let's walk,' I urged.

Carrying our sandals, we trudged along the water's edge holding hands. I looked back at our footprints in the wet sand and imagined they were those of a young Robert and Elizabeth walking the same path. Their images filled my vision.

Ahead of us, Eden spotted an outcrop of rock that offered protection from the sun and wind. He walked towards it, beckoning me to follow, and spread towels on the soft sand. He removed a flask of coffee from his tog bag and opened it, filling two paper cups and handing one to me. I lifted the satchel over my shoulder and put it on the towel. Eden, sitting cross-legged, rolled the cup between his palms. His gaze fell on the satchel and he raised an eyebrow questioningly. I pressed the bronze lock on Robert's satchel and it snapped open, disgorging the letters.

Eden was incredulous. I inhaled deeply to steady my thoughts, choosing my words carefully. 'These letters are from my father whom I never met. You know so little about me, Eden, but when you have read these letters all that will change.'

He held my gaze, his eyes soft and transparent. 'I love you, Emmy nothing will change that.'

I stacked the letters into bundles, ending with the last one that Robert had written to me. Eden reached for an envelope, unfolding the letter inside. Resting his back against the rock he began to read.

Only the cawing of gulls and the ebb and flow of waves breaking on the water's edge disturbed the silence of the world around me, still peaceful.

I steeled myself for his reaction. Eden's expression was inscrutable as he read the letters, his lips moving silently. At times he would look up at me, widen his eyes, or shake his head.

A buttery sun had moved past its zenith when Eden folded the last letter into its envelope and stood up with his back to me stretching his legs. His palms were pressed against his hips, his chin down, absorbed in thought. Then he turned and sat down next to me, drawing me into an embrace. I buried my face in his chest feeling the warmth of his breath on my skin.

'Thank you for sharing Robert's letters with me.' His expression was solemn, yet filled with compassion. Grains of sand clung to his dark lashes. 'Emmy,' he said, his finger tracing a line down my cheek, 'it's time for me to meet your mother.'

I swallowed and jutted out my chin turning away from him. 'You mean Elizabeth?'

'No, Emmy, I mean your mother.' He emphasised the word 'mother'. 'Your parents were selfless and courageous and your mother continues to be.'

'She abandoned me,' I answered, obdurately.

Eden chewed on his bottom lip. In the silence, I saw emotion move in waves across his face.

'Your parents did not abandon you,' he said, slowly. 'They were concerned for your safety and left you in the care of Oumie and Pa until they could return. Robert and Elizabeth yearned for you. They sacrificed their security to achieve their goals. It is a miracle that Elizabeth survived the car bomb.'

He reached for my hand.

'Could it be that your anger is directed at Karel and Miemie? Perhaps they are the ones you feel have abandoned you and you have not yet come to terms with their deaths? You are unleashing your resentment and grief on Elizabeth. She came back into your life at the time Karel died. With Miemie's passing, your life changed, and again when you left Tweefontein. Neither Karel nor Miemie could have prevented these changes. Your heartache is the whip you use to hurt Elizabeth, your mother.'

Eden's words sliced into my heart. A pulse throbbed in my temples. Pent-up grief rose in waves. I sobbed into my hands releasing my pain, my shoulders heaving.

Until Eden rocked me in his arms as though I were a child.

Until my pain subsided.

The sand was warm against my back, the stuttering rhythm of Eden's heartbeat against mine. The silence was filled with words that didn't need speaking. The world stood still, and I surrendered to this moment. I wanted to stay in it forever.

The light was fading when we retraced our footsteps along the water's edge.

I heard Oumie's voice whispering in the wind, the breeze carrying her words back to me. 'My child, we never left you. Our love for you is bound up with Robert's and Elizabeth's and with Eden's. Be happy, child. Pa and I will always be beside you.'

Elizabeth was waiting for me on our balcony. I looked up and waved. Before I climbed out of the jeep, Eden tugged my arm, drawing me back. He was pensive, weighing his words with care. 'You don't know much about me either, Emmy. I would like you and Elizabeth to come for dinner tomorrow night to meet my family. Will you?'

He searched my face for an answer. I nodded, then climbed the stairs towards Elizabeth.

We never did find the fisherman's hut that Robert and Elizabeth had lived in, but it didn't matter. I had pieced together the broken parts of my life and the future beckoned enticingly.

CHAPTER 50

Stars pricked the night sky when Elizabeth and I arrived at Eden's parent's home. There were no streetlights in the leafy suburb of Constantia. Elizabeth took many wrong turns in the darkened avenues but eventually we reached Birdhaven Crescent.

I pressed the buzzer outside latticed iron gates, and they swung open to reveal a brick walkway leading up to the house with its covered veranda. Emerald-green lawns sloped down to a sparkling pool and large white pots filled with flowering shrubs bordered the pathway. An ornate bronze knocker was attached to the front door. Eden and his father had walked down the veranda steps to greet us. Eden's dark hair was smoothed behind his ears, his white open-necked shirt gleamed against his bronzed skin.

'He is so handsome,' I thought, emotion colouring my face. I tugged self-consciously at my floral summer dress and flicked my hair back over my shoulder. Eden threaded his fingers through mine, drawing me towards his father.

'Meet my father, Charles.' He addressed Elizabeth and me, gesturing to a tall, heavyset man with greying temples. Charles was a version of his brother Simon, Jenny's father, but unlike Simon – who had red hair and a beard to match – Charles was cleanshaven with dark hair shot with silver. He had a broad, generous face and lips that curled readily into a smile. I tightened my grip on Eden's hand and took a deep, steadying breath.

"This is my mother, Elizabeth. Meet my mother."

I chose my words carefully, tasting the strangeness of the word 'mother', and rolled my tongue around it.

Elizabeth swung around to face me and her lips parted in a silent 'O'. I held her gaze, both our eyes misting. Eden nodded approvingly and squeezed my hand. Charles, oblivious to the heightened emotion of the moment, threw one arm around Elizabeth and another around me, ushering us indoors.

The warm smells of cooking filled my nostrils and hunger made my stomach grumble. We sipped vintage wine from crystal flutes while exchanging pleasantries. I was beginning to wonder when I would meet Eden's mother. Charles patted his stomach and turned towards the kitchen. 'Zara, is dinner ready?' he called. 'Our guests are hungry.'

She walked towards me with her arms outstretched. She had large almond-shaped eyes and luxuriant dark hair that cascaded around her shoulders. Her flowing yellow dress emphasised her tawny brown skin. She was barefoot.

I was riveted, shock registering on my face. She smiled and then chuckled with amusement at my expression. 'I am Moroccan. Didn't Eden tell you?' She pouted her generous lips.

Before I could answer, a commotion at the front door broke into the moment, and Doron, Eden's brother, burst into the room. He wore cycle shorts and had a towel draped around his neck. He dropped his gym bag onto the floor and stood with his hands on his hips, unabashedly staring at me.

'Wow Eden, you sure choose the prettiest girls.'

Charles chuckled, waving him away. 'Enough of that, young man, wash up and join us for dinner.'

The table groaned with dishes of Moroccan spiced chicken tagine, couscous, pita bread and salads. The atmosphere over dinner was warm and Charles and Zara related their story to a captivated audience, consisting of Elizabeth and myself.

Zara and her family had fled Morocco in the sixties to the safety of Israel. Morocco was marked by state violence and oppression during this period. She had met Charles on a kibbutz where they packed fruit. They married, and Eden and Doron were born on the kibbutz. Charles never stopped hankering after his home in South Africa, but the family could not return until the country became democratic and Zara could be accepted into society.

The Gelbs were enthralled by Elizabeth's description of the role she and Robert had played during the apartheid years and were horrified by the tragedy of Robert's violent death.

'It is a miracle that you survived, Elizabeth. You are a hero for carrying your burden with such dignity.' Charles took Elizabeth's hand in both of his.

Time had passed undetected and it was almost midnight when Elizabeth glanced at her watch, and we rose to leave.

'Do come again,' Zara implored. We both nodded eagerly.

Eden followed us to the car. Out of earshot I whispered to him, 'Why didn't you tell me that your mother was brown-skinned, like mine?'

'Unlike you, I didn't grow up in South Africa and skin colour never mattered – it never affected me. Nor should it you. We are all a part of the same human race.'

I lowered my eyes coyly. 'Your mother is beautiful. You are like her.'

Eden held me close. 'And your mother is a hero to me. You are like her in your resilience. You have come a long way from the shy farm girl I met in Camps Bay to the worldly woman who you now are.'

Elizabeth and I drove home in silence, each lost in thought.

We had found a new family in the Gelbs and, finally, we had found each other.

EPILOGUE

ELIZABETH

Silver and gold strobe lights crisscross the lawns in the garden of Birdhaven Crescent.

It is Emmy's twenty-first birthday and Charles and Zara are hosting a party to celebrate the occasion.

Max stands beside me near the open-air dance floor and we watch in fascination as nubile young bodies twist and turn to Ricky Martin's rendition of 'Living la vita loco'.

I am now Mrs Mendel. Max and I married last year and Emmy and I have relocated from the flat in Rondebosch to his home. I continue to be his assistant and he is still the rock on which I lean for support. Emmy is now the proud owner of the blue second-hand Toyota.

If I close my eyes, I can summon Robert's image, feel his touch, see his smile, the tilt of his head when he speaks. Emmy is so much like him that she keeps his memory alive. When unwelcome thoughts of the car bomb that killed him rise to the front of my mind, I am now able to push them aside.

Max touches my hand, intruding into my thoughts.

'You look beautiful tonight,' he whispers.

I smile. The chartreuse halter-neck dress I wear is an indulgence. The saleslady remarked that the shade emphasised the colour of my eyes thereby crushing all my resistance to purchasing it.

Emmy maintains the tradition and spent her birthday morning with Zelda and Barney in the house on Magnolia Street. They made pancakes and ate them in their fingers around the kitchen table. In this way, Emmy reverts to being a little girl again. Her pink bedroom remains untouched, and she spends many nights there when lectures end late. She is studying for an honours degree and has a heavy workload. I speak to Robert in my mind, assuring him of how proud we are of our daughter.

Barney presents Emmy with a pair of silver earrings. They match the locket she received on her seventh birthday and she is thrilled with the gift. Although she towers over him now, she covers Barney with kisses. She wears the locket which is like the one I wear. Mine still has the picture of baby Emmy in it and, after all the years, it still rests in the hollow of my throat.

Max and I walk over to the table where Thabu and Sipho are engrossed in conversation with Charles and Zara. Sipho draws up chairs and they shift around the table to make space for us. Charles beckons a white-jacketed waiter and canapes are promptly served.

I spot Anna and David Moses at the entrance and wave to them. Having arrived late, they seem bewildered by the large crowd. Between hugs and handshakes, more chairs are drawn up and they settle among us.

The music has changed. Whitney Houston is belting out 'Baby One More Time' and my feet begin to tap. I drag Max onto the dance floor and we join the revellers. I am young again and feel buoyant, lighter than air.

We return to the table to find that Zelda and Barney have joined the party. Barney's walker is parked beside the chair he sits on. We all turn to watch Emmy and Eden on the dance floor, their energy seems boundless. Emmy wears a flowing white dress emphasising her statuesque figure. The dress is shot with a silver thread and she has white gardenias pinned in her hair. The silver earrings, Barney's gift, sparkle against her unblemished skin. She is radiant. I am filled with love and pride.

Emmy and Eden join us at the table. Emmy greets David and Anna joyfully and they become emotional. Memories are fired. They experience flashbacks to a cold winter's night in London when Robert arrives on their doorstep to inform them of Emmy's birth. Together we relive the hopes and heartaches that have catapulted us into this moment.

I glance across the table at Emmy. Her face is flushed with happiness, her hand rests on Eden's arm. Her lips are parted as though to speak. Gardenia petals drift in her hair and I know that I will hold this moment in my heart forever.

The faces around the table blur and fade and I am alone in a tunnel of time and space. The ghosts of Miemie, Karel and Robert appear to me.

'Look around you Libby,' Pa says. 'This is the rainbow nation and you are part of its creation.' Miemie nods. Robert looks directly at me. 'You would do it all again. It was worth it, Elizabeth.'

Then they fade away and I breathe myself into being.

And so it is.

And so it is.

ACKNOWLEDGEMENT

I am deeply grateful to the U3A writing group for their encouragement and support throughout the process of writing this novel. I value our unique friendship.

Thank you: Isa Herring, Maureen Narunsky, Rhona Rom, Beryl Eichenberger and Gwynne Robins for reading my first draft and for your insightful critique.

Thank you Tertius van Eeden. Print on Demand has been a beacon of light guiding me throughout the publishing process.

Thank you Alexia Lawson, editor of note, for your invaluable inspiration and patience with an erratic author.

Percy, Irene, Tony and Linda. You are my constant source of support. Thank you.

Thank you Henry, for always believing in me and for making the impossible seem possible. My love and gratitude always.

Amanda, Tamara and Pablo. Thank you for your unwavering and unconditional love and for your tolerance in listening to my stories – again.

And to the heroines of those stories; Bertha, Margaret, Ellalou, Susan Reeve and Gillian.

This one's for you.

In memory of Margie Fortuin.

ABOUT THE AUTHOR

ANGELA MILLER-ROTHBART was born and raised in Paarl, South Africa. She is an entrepreneur, businesswoman, advanced Toastmaster and voice over artist. She is a mother of two daughters and has a grandson. Currently, she lives in Sea Point with her husband Henry.

This is her second novel.

AUTHORS PAGE: *printondemand.co.za/angela-rothbart*
BLOG: *printondemand.co.za/writers-journey*

www.ingramcontent.com/pod-product-compliance
Lightning Source LLC
Chambersburg PA
CBHW022008100426
42736CB00041B/1038